KEEP YOURSELF SAFE

A GUIDE FOR REAL ESTATE PROFESSIONALS IN CONNECTICUT

DONATO SINISI

Training is not a luxury, it's a necessity. Anyone who tells you otherwise are simply deluding themselves.

-DAN SINISI

<u>Important</u>

This book serves as general informative guidelines and should not be construed as legal advice. It is important that you check your local and state laws as well as employer policies.

Be Safe!

Table of Contents

Introduction

Every occupation has safety and security concerns and the Real Estate profession is no exception. Just like most of us, we heavily depend on our local law enforcement, fire and EMS to respond and handle our emergencies or issues to our safety. If your agency is located in a more urban area, private security officers may be assigned to your office or building. Keep in mind that law enforcement is more reactive rather than proactive, although they are increasing their proactive stance with some great results. Realistically however, they can't be everywhere at once and simply don't have the manpower. Employing private security is an alternative that the agency may not, due to budgetary concerns, afford the cost of hiring security officers. Simply put, your personal safety is just that – *your* personal safety!

Real Estate Agents have a unique job in that it often requires them to meet with potential clients or buyers alone, whether at the office or at a property. Either way, you must be vigilant, be prepared and always have a plan!

Many of you may not have received any formal training in self-defense or diffusing a situation. This book is designed for real estate professionals in the State of Connecticut to give you the opportunity to be both proactive and reactive to your personal safety. However, outside of Connecticut specific information, this book may be applied to other jurisdictions as well.

As you will note throughout this book, I continue to stress that your personal safety is just that – *your* personal safety!

Your safety comes first! As we say in the Public Safety profession – we all want to go home at the end of the day to our friends and families.

I truly hope that you will find *"Keep Yourself Safe: A Guide for Real Estate Professionals"* to be informative, interesting and thought provoking.

Sexual Harassment

This book is not intended to train on sexual harassment nor should this be construed as legal advice. Generally speaking, Human Resources or your employer will cover this and should have written policies specific to your location and geographic area. However, there are a few things you should be aware of as an employee or manager.

All employers and businesses have a sexual harassment policy written within their policies and procedures. It is strongly recommended that you read it carefully and adhere to it.

Sexual harassment is defined as any "unwelcome sexual advances or requests for sexual favors or any conduct of a sexual nature when conduct is made explicitly or implicitly as a condition of employment, submitting to or rejecting such conduct adversely affects your employment status, and/or such conduct interferes with work performance or creates an intimidating, hostile, or offensive work environment."

There are some employers and/or clients who specifically prohibit dating co-workers for various reasons. Proceed with caution!

Remember, sexual harassment is not only a violation of company policy but it is against the law!

Persons who engage in sexual harassment may find themselves with disciplinary actions, civil litigation, and criminal penalties.

Sexual harassment conduct should be reported immediately to your supervisor or human resources representative. Connecticut law requires that a formal complaint be filed with the Commission on Human Rights and Opportunities within 180 days of the date when the alleged harassment occurred.

Policies and Procedures

We all want to feel safe at work and many of us don't even give it a second thought until, unfortunately, an incident occurs. We talk about it, make proposals and even get estimates for upgraded security features or services – after the fact. Most of the time there is no follow through, perhaps because of budget constraints or a lack of willpower or inconvenience to staff or management. From our experience the latter appears to be the front runner. It's for this reason you have to take your personal safety seriously. Whether you are in your office, at home, in transit or anywhere else, your safety is of the utmost importance.

For those of you who are employed in a real estate office or building, you should understand that the employer has an obligation to do everything "reasonable" to keep you safe while on the property. In a Court of Law, reasonable is the burden of proof in which an average person in the same circumstances would do the same thing in place of the employer, property owner, or person. It's in the property owner's best interest to provide a safe environment due to liability and continued business operations.

Once thought of as regulating only industrial sites, the Occupational Safety & Health Administration actually regulates safety in all workplaces, although not every profession or industry has its own OSHA standard. There are currently no specific standards for workplace violence. One thing that applies everywhere is the General Duty Clause which states in part that, *"Each employer shall furnish to each of his employees employment and a place of employment which are free from recognized hazards that are causing or are likely to cause death or serious physical harm to his employees and Each employee shall comply with occupational safety and health standards and all rules, regulations, and orders issued pursuant to this Act which are applicable to his own actions and conduct."*

All companies should have written policies and procedures available either directly to the employee (i.e. a handbook, digital device, etc.) or be available at all times in the workplace. These policies cover many different areas of the business operations and code of conduct. Included within these procedures should be guidelines that cover safety, security, prevention and response protocols. Management and employees alike should have a good understanding of the options available to them with regards to facility safety and the safety of its employees. Keep in mind that company policies and procedures can't conflict with state statutes. Rather they should compliment them.

Private Security officers (private citizens providing protective services) receive their authority from two sources:

1. State Statutes
2. Employer Polices

You can't have one without the other.

Likewise, *private citizens* must adhere to the same standards.

You will see one of Sound Training Group's policies and procedures. In this example, these procedures are directed to students and participants who attend our training. We have separate policies that cover test taking, training locations and others. You will notice the date the policy was issued and the "review" date. Policies and procedures must be periodically reviewed and updated for changing operations and circumstances. We recommend that policies be updated at least yearly to reflect changing times and to be current. Be sure you know who the target audience is and state it.

A policy should include a brief summary of why one is needed, the benefits and resolutions.

The main part of the policy should include steps or guidelines to address certain situations and how to rectify them. Keep in mind the policies should be clear and convey your message thoroughly so there is no question about how to handle an issue. It is important to remember that policies are fluid as management and staff may interpret it differently.

In the case of personal safety in the office or in the field, be sure your policies reflect proactive, reactive and communication steps. It is strongly recommended that emergencies such as fires and workplace violence among others be addressed separately as individual policies so there is no confusion. In many cases, it's not a "one size fits all" and must be treated as such accordingly.

It is important that policies also address sanctions if the rules are not followed. Safety is everyone's concern and complying with company policies is important.

Sound Training Group LLP Stamford, Connecticut 06901	POLICIES & PROCEDURES		
Title: **General Rules - Training**			Policy #: 14-01
Date Issued: October 2014	Date Reviewed: September 2015	Approved: **Donato Sinisi, Alan F. Shaw, Partners**	Page 1 of 1
Revised: **October 2015**			
Distribution: **Students / Participants**			

EXAMPLE

POLICY: To ensure that all participants / students comply with Sound Training Group LLP training and education etiquettes so all may benefit, learn and apply.

PROCEDURE:

1. This is a serious course of instruction and should be treated as such.
2. Do not text or answer phone calls during instruction. If you must use your cell phone or device, leave the room. Material covered during your absence may not be re-covered. Questions related to the material may be found on an examination.
3. There will be periodic breaks.
4. Absolutely no horseplay!
5. If you need to use the restroom, please leave quietly without disturbing the other students.
6. This course material is copyright pending – <u>do not copy, distribute, sell, re-brand or otherwise engage in the commercial use of this course material.</u>
7. Sound Training Group LLP, its partners, employees, vendors, agents, consultants, etc. do not guarantee that having completed this course of instruction, you will become gainfully employed, promoted, or otherwise achieve your desired position.
8. Students are encouraged to interact during the course of instruction. However, questions or statements should focus on the instruction at hand. Be respectful of other's opinions.
9. Absolutely no use of obscenities or obscene gestures! After one warning, you may be asked to leave the class with no monies returned or a refund.
10. Once the course has initiated, there will be no refunds – no exceptions. Please be sure you are qualified with the State and/or employer to take this course.
11. Sound Training Group LLP, its partners, employees, vendors, agents, consultants, etc. are held harmless if, for whatever reason, you are unable to obtain a license, credential, certification, CEU's or other documentation.

_____ I agree to abide by the above General Rules and Housekeeping items.

_____ I do not agree to abide by the above General Rules and Housekeeping items.

Signature: _____

Print Full Name: _____

Date: _____

Trespassing on Private Property

Trespassing means the unlawful intrusion of one's property which is owned and/or maintained by such person(s) or controlled by such person(s) who have a lawful right to occupy the property.

In the State of Connecticut, the following statutes apply:

Sec. 53a-107. Criminal trespass in the first degree: Class A misdemeanor. (a) A person is guilty of criminal trespass in the first degree when: (1) Knowing that such person is not licensed or privileged to do so, such person enters or remains in a building or any other premises after an order to leave or not to enter personally communicated to such person by the owner of the premises or other authorized person; or (2) such person enters or remains in a building or any other premises in violation of a restraining order issued pursuant to section 46b-15 or a protective order issued pursuant to section 46b-38c, 54-1k or 54-82r by the Superior Court. (b) Criminal trespass in the first degree is a class A misdemeanor.

Sec. 53a-108. Criminal trespass in the second degree: Class B misdemeanor. (a) A person is guilty of criminal trespass in the second degree when, knowing that he is not licensed or privileged to do so, he enters or remains in a building. (b) Criminal trespass in the second degree is a class B misdemeanor.

Sec. 53a-109. Criminal trespass in the third degree: Class C misdemeanor. (a) A person is guilty of criminal trespass in the third degree when, knowing that he is not licensed or privileged to do so: (1) He enters or remains in premises which are posted in a manner prescribed by law or reasonably likely to come to the attention of intruders, or fenced or otherwise enclosed in a manner designed to exclude intruders, or which belong to the state and are appurtenant to any state institution;

or (2) he enters or remains in any premises for the purpose of hunting, trapping or fishing. (b) Criminal trespass in the third degree is a class C misdemeanor.

Sec. 53a-110a. Simple trespass: Infraction. (a) A person is guilty of simple trespass when, knowing that he is not licensed or privileged to do so, he enters any premises without intent to harm any property. (b) Simple trespass is an infraction.

Sec. 53a-110d. Simple trespass of railroad property: Infraction. (a) A person is guilty of simple trespass of railroad property when, knowing that such person is not licensed or privileged to do so, such person enters or remains on railroad property without lawful authority or the consent of the railroad carrier. (b) Simple trespass of railroad property is an infraction.

Sec. 53a-110. Affirmative defenses to criminal trespass. It shall be an affirmative defense to prosecution for criminal trespass that: (1) The building involved in the offense was abandoned; or (2) the premises, at the time of the entry or remaining, were open to the public and the actor complied with all lawful conditions imposed on access to or remaining in the premises; or (3) the actor reasonably believed that the owner of the premises, or a person empowered to license access thereto, would have licensed him to enter or remain, or that he was licensed to do so.

Business owners, by virtue of commerce, must keep a balance between safety and security and allowing prospective clients to enter the premises to conduct business. It's understandable that business owners, in most cases, will have an "open door policy" whereas clients may enter the facility or property without impediment, thus lies where to tip the balance and why it's important for the individual to care for their own personal safety.

Most facilities employ "No Soliciting" signage at the entrance but rarely do we see a "No Trespassing" sign. Many businesses make every effort to welcome potential clients to their offices.

All businesses have the right to legally post signage indicating they are giving notice to anyone who might be entering the property the right to search bags and to give such persons the opportunity to leave before further entering the property. With that in mind, here are a few things to keep in mind:

When Notice Is Given:

It specifically concerns a controlled environment, open or closed property, facilities, schools, etc.

Examples of Notice Given: In the form of written signage at the property line, entrance to property, entrance gate, property marker, guard house, gate house, office, lobby or any other place in which the private property has control of the business or controlled property. The Notice, when properly employed, must clearly inform all those entering to give the person an opportunity to change their mind and not enter the property.

Consent:

When Notices are properly posted and displayed, any individual who enters the property has given "implied consent" at the point of entering. Implied consent is used at various types of properties including federal buildings, courthouses, manufacturers, government properties, schools, healthcare facilities and businesses. In all cases, the property owner will either give notice by posting signage throughout the property for external customers or upon being hired the employers will give notice to employees that they may conduct "reasonable" search of their belongings as they leave the property to ensure they are not leaving with company assets. In many cases, businesses, schools and healthcare facilities have a clear "No Drugs" and "No Weapons" policy and when proper notice is given, may conduct random searches of lockers, vehicles, bags, packages, briefcases or any other container-like items.

The chance of real estate professionals employing any type of search is at best minimal. However, this will give you an idea of what proactive options you have prior to anyone setting foot in your office. It is for these very reasons we encourage written policies and procedures to address issues such as these.

Your office or facility is your "castle" so to speak and you should feel as safe as possible. Think of the property line as your first line of defense. Although posting signage may not deter all would-be wrong doers, some may think twice and turn around. You have to show everyone, even clients, that you take safety and security seriously. Begin with the perimeter of the property. Depending on the property layout, a metal chain link fence no lower than six feet in height is really a good option with a controlled gate accessible by a remote or call button. Most people will walk away especially if the fence also encloses a parking area. No parking signs such as "Private Property" and "Authorized Parking Only – All Other Will Be Towed at Owner's Expense" will generally dissuade anyone from not only parking on the property but attempting access to the building. From the outside, the facility must portray a perception of security measures.

Placing a receptionist or security officer in a lobby is another defense layer. Everyone walking into the facility should stop at the desk to announce themselves and state who they are meeting with. The receptionist should then call the real estate professional to confirm that in fact the visitor has an appoint and may further enter the facility.

Identification Badges:

Most businesses do not require visitors to present identification upon entering the facility and may ask the person to sign a guest book instead. The problem here is that the business is completely relying on the honesty of that person to write down their real information, otherwise known as a "self-initiated process." The business should take into consideration of requiring identification and if possible to make a copy. If no copies can be made or the visitor refuses to either present identification, the person may have no alternative but to leave the premises. For this to occur however, written policies have to be in place and notice must be given. In this case signage at the desk should indicate your policy.

I recommend using a badge system for all visitors. Badges are inexpensive yet effective in distinguishing visitors on the property. You can customize them to your liking and design. Outside of having them made professionally, which can be cost prohibitive, badges can be made in the office. Basic supplies include paper, a printer, a laminate machine or plastic sleeves and clips. These supplies are generally available in office supply stores.

Below are a few examples and badge types from a local business employing a badge system for contractors and visitors. You will note the simplicity of the design which only includes the name of the business, title of "visitor," and a number. As stated before you can customize it.

(Front)

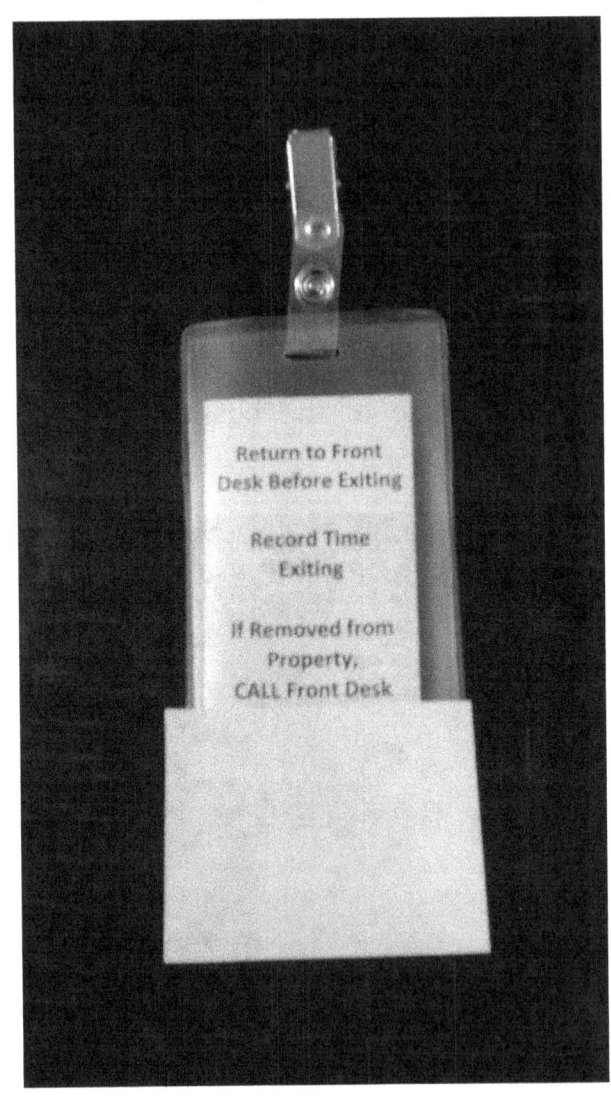

(Back)

(For confidentiality, the name of the business has been covered)

BE SURE TO GET THE BADGES BACK AS THE VISITORS LEAVE!!

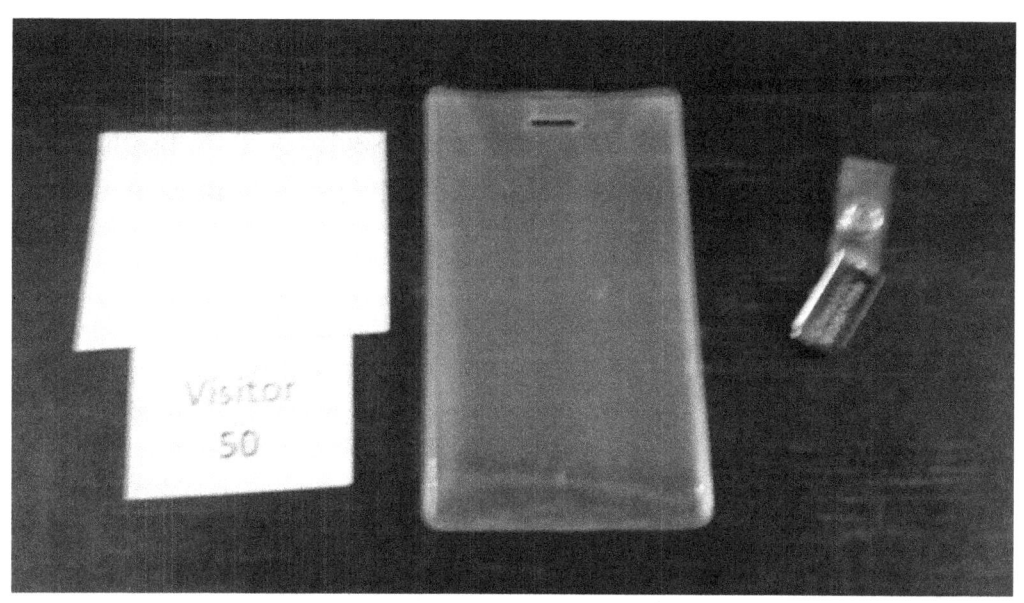

In offices where there is no receptionist or desk, visitors are often left to the "self-initiated" process and find themselves, purposely or not, wandering throughout the facility with no form of control. Security precautions therefore must be stepped up. Everyone has the responsibility to challenge anyone who appears to be "lost" or "misguided."

Restrooms:

Another scenario which commonly occurs is the visitor entering the facility and although has no appointment, asks to use the restroom. From a respectful standpoint, it's not an unusual request but from a security standpoint, a few things should be going through your mind before you decide whether or not you allow access.

First, this person does not have an appointment. What this person says and what he/she does is something else. Does this person have criminal intent? Is this person going to use the restroom as a staging area for any criminal activity?

Second, the business may be setting a precedent for others to follow, thus inviting other potential criminal actors. In this case, signage and written policies are very important. A sign that clearly states "No Public Restrooms" will work well. It's important to note that you can't simply allow some people and not others, especially when notice is given, access to the restroom as the business could themselves be on the wrong end of discrimination lawsuit.

If you do allow access to the restroom, a staff member should post themselves in the area of the restroom and wait for the person to exit to make sure they leave the premises. Once the person has left, check the restroom for anything left behind that may appear suspicious such as a hand bag, backpack, etc. You never know if an explosive device or other material was just planted. It's a good idea to keep the empty restroom locked at all times so there is no "double backing."

Surveillance Cameras

The installation of Closed Circuit Television Cameras (CCTVs) is perhaps the best, practical and least expensive option. I recommend both exterior and interior CCTVs to cover most if not all the property. From a proactive standpoint include signage indicating there are surveillance cameras for their protection.

Recorded video and monitoring accomplishes several things:

➢ Actively monitor who is in the office or building.
➢ Monitor for medical emergencies.
➢ Aid law enforcement during investigations of persons or property.
➢ Can be introduced into Court to dispute alleged false accusations.

Placement of CCTVs:

Ideally every corner of the property both inside and out would be covered under surveillance. Many businesses simply can't afford the cost of multiple cameras everywhere. In this case cameras have to be placed in strategic locations and areas of value.

Strategic Locations:

> All common areas.
> Lobby areas.
> Elevator hallway/vestibule locations (also include interior of cars).
> Facility entry and exit points (emergency exits included).
> Interior stairwells.
> Computer server room doors.
> Parking garage/areas.

Places of Value:

> Meeting rooms.
> Rooms or areas where confidential documentation is kept.
> Vault or other secured area where money or bank drafts are kept.
> Other areas where management and staff feel surveillance is appropriate.

Important!

CCTVs may not be placed in the following areas:

> Locker rooms.
> Restrooms.
> Individual offices.

There are many types of cameras with various abilities. These days, individuals can purchase a complete CCTV set from many of the big box stores as well as specialized locations. They have become relatively inexpensive and more portable. Many have motion sensor capabilities built in. The property does not necessarily need a server room and may opt to monitor activities via the web anytime from the office, home or on your phone.

One important issue I find with businesses who employ CCTVs is that there is no one dedicated to monitoring the cameras. In fact, the monitor(s) are placed in a different room out of view of others. It is understandable that businesses do not want to give the impression the property is unsafe. However the public, at minimum, must have a perception of security. There is a false sense of security that the cameras are recording and no one gives it a second thought until something occurs. It is important that someone, perhaps a security officer, a receptionist or an administrative person keep a watchful eye. It would simply defeat the purpose of having CCTVs deployed if someone can't monitor activities and be proactive.

It's also recommended that property owners seek the advice of a security consultant who will be able address your specific layout and issues.

Be sure that at least two people are familiar with how the CCTVs operate, record and playback.

"Dummy" cameras have increasingly become popular as a very inexpensive alternative to the real thing. As the name suggests, they are not real cameras. They are made to look real including a flashing red light indicator and a cable. Set up only takes a few minutes. Trained professionals and wrong doers can easily spot the difference. The perception of a recording CCTV is all it takes sometimes to change people's behaviors.

The downside to dummy cameras of course is they are not monitoring activities, recording or will not be able to assist in any investigation. Law enforcement generally frown on these because of the false sense of security and offer no assistance should they be called in to investigate a crime.

Portable Radios/Cell Phones:

I always encourage staff to have at least one pair of portable radios at the office. They have become relatively inexpensive and are usually sold in pairs in big box stores or online. They should always be on charge and used if there is a power failure, cell phones cease to work or there is an emergency where communication is vital. They should be tested periodically to make sure they are functional. Do not purchase the same radios that children are likely playing with and found in toy stores – the frequency is not the same and will not perform to the standard you need in the event of an incident.

Be sure to use the portable radios sparingly. It is very important that "plain language" be used when communicating with others. Many people will not understand police "jargon."

Remember, the most important assets that need to be protected are people!

Fire Safety

As a volunteer Fire/Police Officer, I have responded to many fires and rescues. Each incident is unique. Even with all the training, you really don't know what you will encounter. At minimum we should all be prepared and be able to respond to life threatening conditions until emergency responders arrive.

Responding to Smoke Conditions and/or Structure Fires:

Encountering or responding to a smoke conditions can be a very dangerous endeavor. All employers should have written policies on how to respond to this type of emergency. Be prepared and know the property's policies ahead of time!

With some exceptions, most facilities will evacuate the facility if a fire alarm is activated or a fire is reported. It is important the evacuation is quick and orderly and you are familiar with escape routes. Escape routes are generally posted on the walls throughout the facility on all floors and also designate secondary routes. Once firefighters arrive, a Security Officer (if available) may be asked to escort them to the location of activation. Staff should be prepared in assisting emergency responders with explaining the layout of the facility, who may still be inside, and other investigatory questions.

Fire Extinguishers:

Staff should be trained on how and when to use fire extinguishers and the types that exist. In most cases, fire extinguishers and fire pull stations are located either inside or outside the stairwells, inside or outside mechanical rooms and other areas of the facility or grounds where fire suppression may be necessary including entrance and exit points. Fire pull stations are generally placed in strategic areas such as egress points. The idea is that as people evacuate the building, someone will activate the alarm before exiting the facility. Although most facilities will employ a fire maintenance contractor to inspect the extinguishers on a yearly basis, it is strongly recommended that designated staff check them once a month in their travels to be sure the gauge pressure is at the designated level and there are no physical defects. Make notes of which extinguishers you checked with date and time and what condition you found them in. Immediately report defective suppression equipment and take them out of service! Important – be sure fire escape routes, hallways and doors are not blocked to prevent egress!!

Important – be sure fire escape routes, hallways and doors are not blocked to prevent egress!!

Types of Fire Extinguishers:

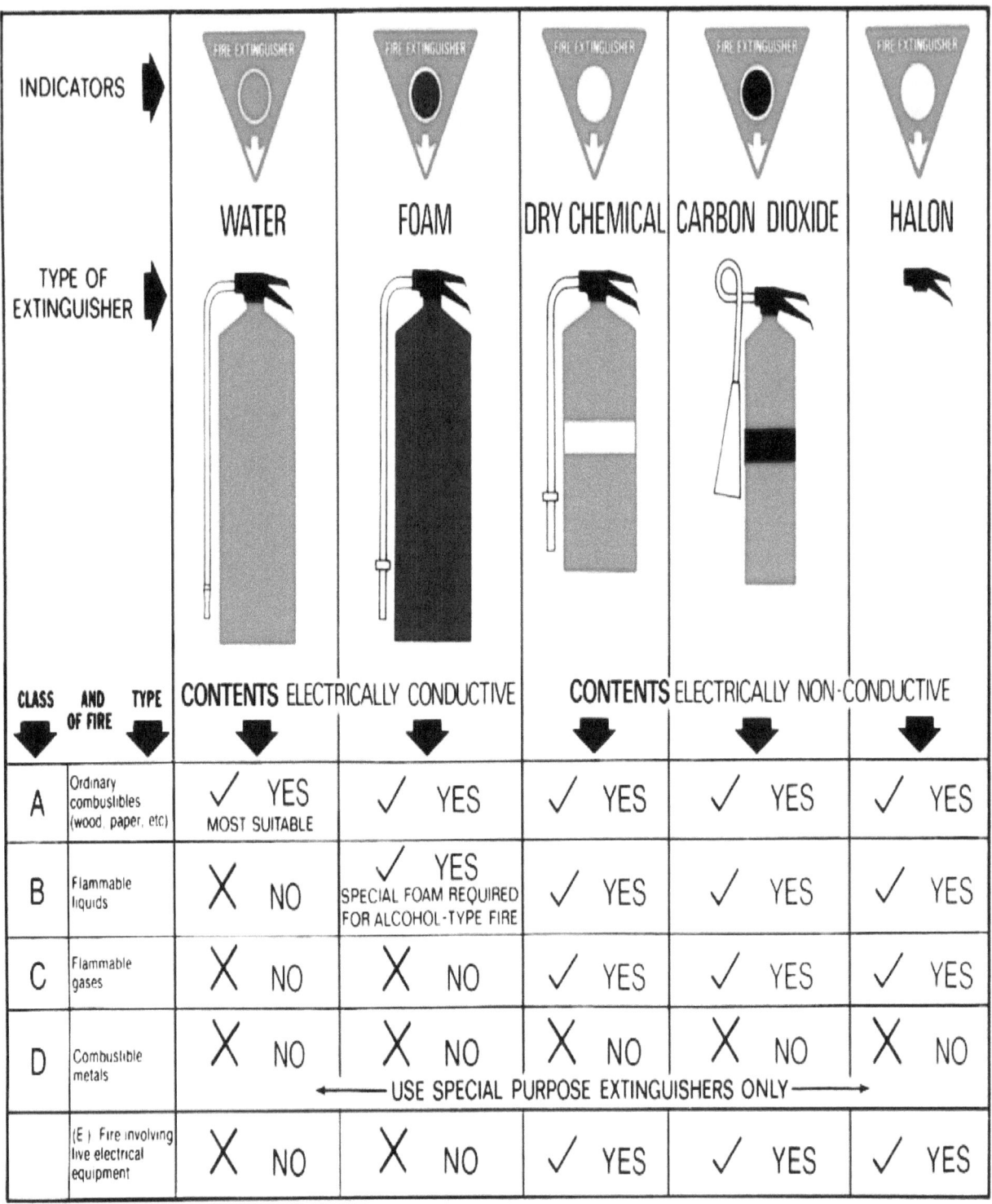

CLASS AND TYPE OF FIRE		WATER (CONTENTS ELECTRICALLY CONDUCTIVE)	FOAM (CONTENTS ELECTRICALLY CONDUCTIVE)	DRY CHEMICAL (CONTENTS ELECTRICALLY NON-CONDUCTIVE)	CARBON DIOXIDE (CONTENTS ELECTRICALLY NON-CONDUCTIVE)	HALON (CONTENTS ELECTRICALLY NON-CONDUCTIVE)
A	Ordinary combustibles (wood, paper, etc)	✓ YES MOST SUITABLE	✓ YES	✓ YES	✓ YES	✓ YES
B	Flammable liquids	✗ NO	✓ YES SPECIAL FOAM REQUIRED FOR ALCOHOL-TYPE FIRE	✓ YES	✓ YES	✓ YES
C	Flammable gases	✗ NO	✗ NO	✓ YES	✓ YES	✓ YES
D	Combustible metals	✗ NO	✗ NO	✗ NO	✗ NO	✗ NO
			← USE SPECIAL PURPOSE EXTINGUISHERS ONLY →			
	(E) Fire involving live electrical equipment	✗ NO	✗ NO	✓ YES	✓ YES	✓ YES

Most facilities will deploy the ABC type. This is generally a multi-purpose extinguisher. Be sure to use the correct extinguisher for the appropriate type of fire.

Halon suppression systems are generally located in mechanical and computer server rooms. If an alarm is activated within these areas and you are inside, you must immediately leave the area once the Halon suppression begins!! Halon deprives oxygen which helps in the suppression of the affected alarm area Therefore it is imperative you evacuate or you could become a casualty!

As a rule of thumb, you should not attempt to douse a fire if you believe one (1) fire extinguisher will not suppress it. Rather, evacuate the area and follow proper protocols.

Should you decide to put out a fire, taking into consideration all of the above, be sure you are using the correct fire extinguisher and follow the "PASS" rule:

> **Pull:** Pull the pin of the fire extinguisher.
> **Aim:** Aim the nozzle of the extinguisher at the **BASE** of the fire.
> **Squeeze:** Squeeze the handles together.
> **Sweep:** Sweep the hose at the base of the fire left to right until the fire is suppressed or the extinguisher is empty.

Always be sure to not corner yourself and have an opening, doorway or escape route readily available!!

Perhaps the best way to remember fire and evacuation procedures is to employ "RACE:"

> **Rescue:** If it can be accomplished safely!!
> **Alarm:** Report emergency situations to emergency responders via 911 and alert the facility staff - have as much information as possible!
> **Contain:** Close doors behind you.
> **Extinguish:** Put out fires according to above steps if it can be done safely!

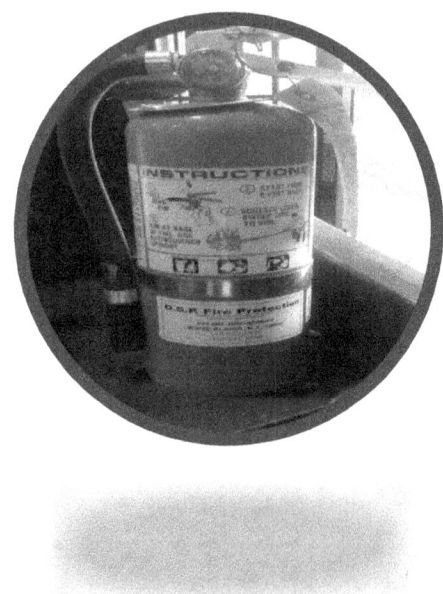

It's very important to treat every single fire alarm activation as if it were the real deal! Do not assume based on past experience that it is just another alarm activation and continue with what you are doing. The one time you ignore it will be the time something is happening. Evacuating the facility should be second nature. Be sure facility policies cover where you are to exit from and where to meet once evacuated.

Many facilities utilize "Fire Wardens." These are pre-designated individuals who, during an incident, make sure other staff members are following proper protocols, follow directions and evacuate safely. Be sure to check in with the Warden once you have reached your meeting place to be accounted for.

Be sure everyone is familiar with the location of where to meet after evacuating to get a head count!

Hazardous Materials:

Chances that real estate agents will encounter and clean up a Hazardous Material incident is almost zero. Common household items such as cleaners, laundry detergent, hand soaps, bleach as well as machine oil, vehicle motor liquids and other facility items are classified as chemicals and are in fact hazardous.

Specialized training in HazMat is required to become a technician and clean up spills or handle chemicals. Healthcare, warehouses and other locations where chemicals are stored usually have their own trained on site staff to deal with such events and will call emergency responders if the spill is more than one (1) gallon. Generally, all training must be compliant with Federal and state Occupational Safety and Health Administration and well as Federal and state Department of Transportation rules. There are a number of hours that must be completed in addition to specific equipment familiarization, decontamination and proper response.

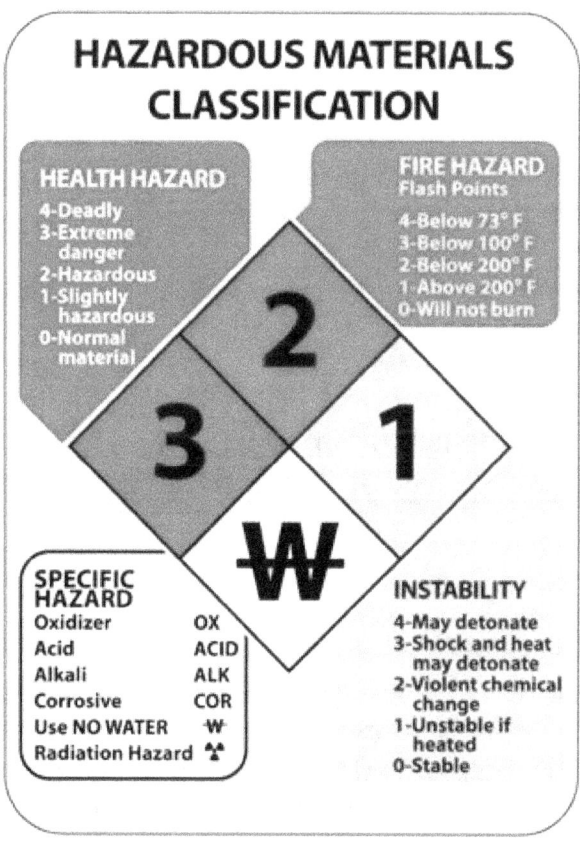

Training:

There are three levels of HazMat responders each with their own unique training requirements and certifications:

> Hazwoper (Hazardous Waste Operations and Emergency Response) 40: (40 hours) Required for workers who perform activities that expose or potentially expose them to hazardous substances.
> Hazwoper 24: (24 hours)Required for employees visiting an uncontrolled Hazardous Waste Operation mandated by the government. Many hospital security and facilities staff receive this level of training.
> Hazwoper 8: Awareness level (8 hours) - most common level of training recommended for safety professionals at any location with stored chemicals. Also used as refresher training which meets the OSHA 29 CFR (Code of Federal Regulations) 1910.120 for eight (8) hour annual refresher training for workers at hazardous waste sites.

It's very important that you be sure that you are medically fit to handle such tasks. Depending at which level you have been trained and certified. You may be fit-tested for masks and suits.

I am very familiar with the how the body responds to suits and masks having been A HazMat Technician for a number of years. Being fully encapsulated will definitely make you perspire and some people may even experience claustrophobia. It's strongly suggested you receive medical clearance from your personal or employer physician.

Hazmat Protective Clothing is Classified as Either Level A, B, C, or D, Based Upon the Degree of Protection They Provide:

Level A;

The highest level of protection against chemicals, gases, vapors and other substances. It requires full encapsulation and the use of an SCBA (Self Contained Breathing Apparatus) or SAR (Supplied Air Respirator) with escape cylinder. In addition it requires wearing chemical resistant gloves and boots specially taped at all seams. The SCBA is worn inside the suit as well as a two-way radio and receiver.

Level B:

Level B protection requires protective clothing (including SCBA) that provides protection against splashes from hazardous chemicals. The SCBA can be worn on the inside our outside of the suit. If worn outside, it is not vapor resistant. The wearing of chemical resistant gloves and boots, taped at seams are also required for protection as well as two-way radios.

Level C:

The protective clothing worn is the same as Level B with the exception that it allows for the use of other respiratory equipment other than the SCBA. Donning this level, the Officer should know what the chemical is and be able to measure it. It can't be used where there is little or no oxygen.

Level D:

This level does not protect you from chemical exposure and should be used only when there is no possibility of chemical contact. All that is needed is a pair of coveralls, chemical resistant boots or other routine protection worn a daily basis such as a lab coat.

Your wardrobe would be considered Level D for this purpose.

If you encounter a hazardous materials situation remember:

- Approach the scene from a safe distance first!
- Notify other personnel of what you observe with as much information as possible.
- Be sure to remain uphill and upwind!
- Depending on your level of training and available equipment, booms may be placed down to stop the flow of the spill from reaching sewers and water lines.
- **DO NOT ATTEMPT TO CLEAN UP THE CHEMICAL ALONE AND WITHOUT PROPER EQUIPMENT AND TRAINING!**
- If the spill is beyond facility capabilities, notify emergency responders.
- Document incident.

Firefighting and HazMat are not your careers. However, every attempt is made to give you as much information as possible in keeping with your safety!!

"Train until it becomes second nature because your personal safety matters."

Dan Sinisi

Suspicious Packages

All businesses receive packages and envelopes in the course of a work day. Most of us will open an envelope or package without giving any thought to what is inside or who it may be from.

Like most businesses, there are a few unhappy clients or customers who in the heat of their anger and disappointment will wish harm on you or the business. Many of these threats do not come to fruition but we have to be aware of the potential and keep our safety in mind in a proactive way.

Larger companies employ mailroom employees that are trained to be observant for packages and envelopes that do not conform to the standard shipping requirements. Some companies go as far as deploying scanning and X-ray equipment to determine if the received items are safe before further processing.

In lieu of this expensive endeavor, there are things you can do to safeguard yourself and the facility.

When accepting or receiving packages and envelopes:

- Closely examine the package or envelope for foreign markings, airmail markings or "special delivery" labels.
- Look for excessive postage or no postage at all or unusual stamping. Perpetrators will often do this to make sure package arrives with no chance of "return to sender."
- Lack of a return address.
- Return address that does not correspond to postal service stamps.
- Information on package or envelope is not familiar with person receiving it.
- Item addressed to a title only rather than a name.
- Newspaper and magazine word clippings used instead of typed or printed information.
- Poor penmanship and misspelled common words.
- Special handling instructions such as "Confidential," "Personal," "Addressee Only," etc.

Additional things to look for:

- ➢ Unnecessary drawings or words that might distract you.
- ➢ An irregular shaped package or envelope, bulky, lopsided, etc.
- ➢ Package or envelope gives off a strange odor.
- ➢ Package appears to be discolored, oily or has stains.
- ➢ You are not expecting a package.
- ➢ Protruding items such as wires, tinfoil or other unusual materials.
- ➢ Excessive use of tape, packing material, strings, etc.

I want to clarify these are indicators to look for and does not necessarily mean there is anything suspicious. However, if any of these indicators ARE present, you should diligently investigate further.

You should start by asking yourself if a package is actually expected. Do you know who it is from? If you are still not sure, verify the return address. If this does not resolve your suspicions, notify law enforcement.

It's important that you do not open up any package or envelope that you believe is suspicious! Many of these packages are triggered upon opening and may disperse powders, nails, weapons of mass destruction (WMDs), or other items and substances. Suspicious packages should be left at its current location and the area secured to prevent others with inadvertently moving it and then evacuate the area.

It is vital that the facility or office have written policies and procedures with protocols and response plans!

Additional safety and security measures should be taken with this or any other incident. As with fire safety procedures, there should be individuals pre-designated to lead in evacuation efforts while emergency responders are en route.

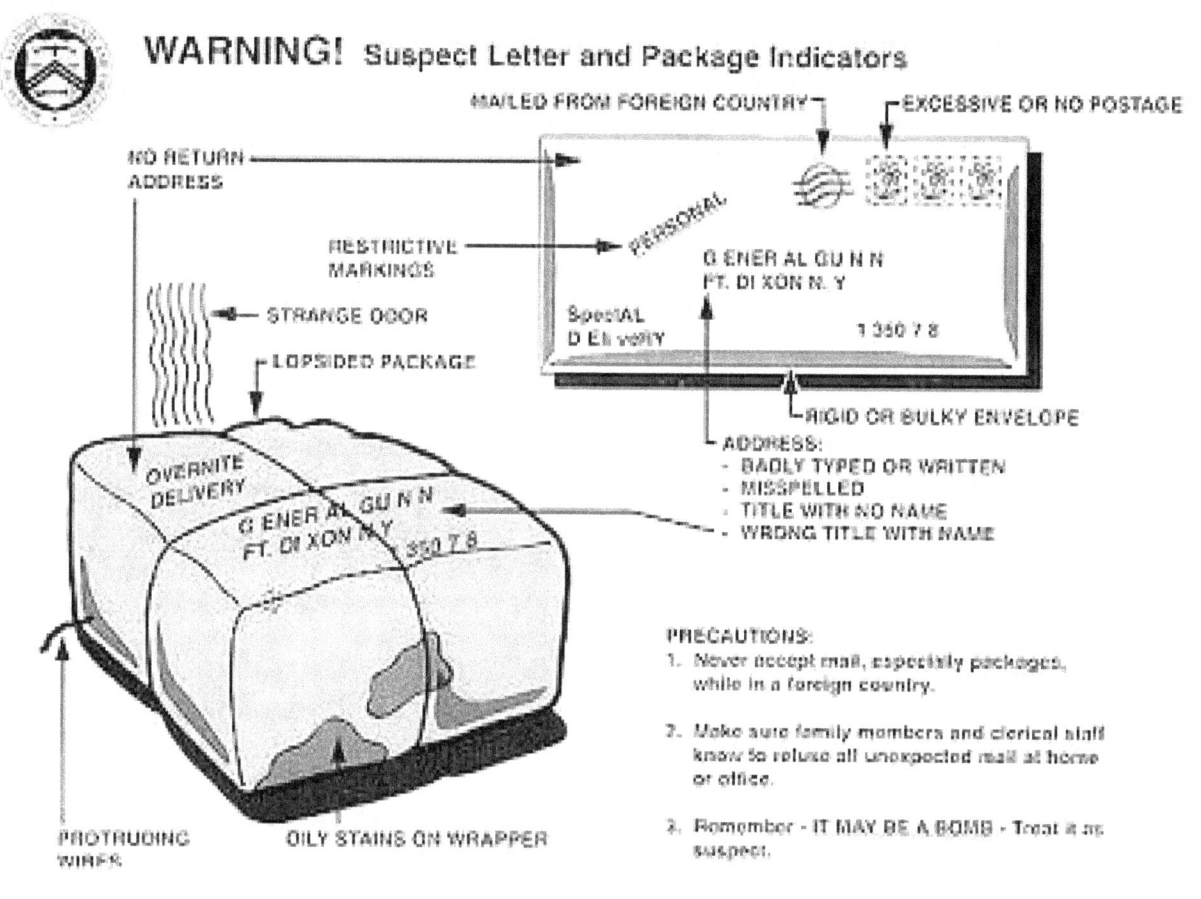

(Courtesy Federal Bureau of Investigation)

If there is an explosion:

➢ A member of the pre-designated team or alternate designee should immediately contact 911.

➢ Find cover or shelter. Bombers will sometimes use a secondary explosive device for responding emergency services or other persons.

Bomb Threat

Periodically, businesses and employers will receive a bomb threat, generally over the telephone or perhaps via social media, notes, etc. It is very important that you take each threat seriously and follow all protocols outlined in your company's procedures which will include evacuating the area Additionally, attempt to keep the caller on the phone, if applicable, as long as possible and obtain as much information as you can. You can use a checklist similar to the one attached here as a guide.

It is essential that you cooperate with law enforcement and fire during this incident. Stay calm, focused and follow all instructions.

Do not use your cell phone to communicate as this may cause the possible detonation of the bomb, if one exists. If the "all clear" is given, you may use your phone or device to communicate with others. If a bomb is located, do not be a hero – comply with requests to leave!

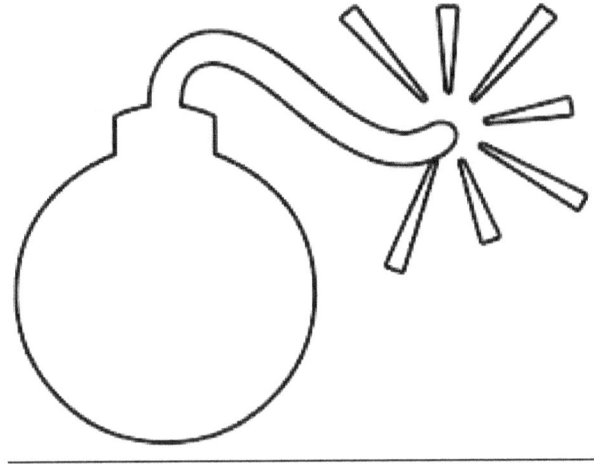

On the following page you will see a standard bomb threat call procedure form from the U.S. Department of Homeland Security. You should familiarize yourself with this form in the event a suspicious call is received.

BOMB THREAT CALL PROCEDURES

Most bomb threats are received by phone. Bomb threats are serious until proven otherwise. Act quickly, but remain calm and obtain information with the checklist on the reverse of this card.

If a bomb threat is received by phone:

1. Remain calm. Keep the caller on the line for as long as possible. DO NOT HANG UP, even if the caller does.
2. Listen carefully. Be polite and show interest.
3. Try to keep the caller talking to learn more information.
4. If possible, write a note to a colleague to call the authorities or, as soon as the caller hangs up, immediately notify them yourself.
5. If your phone has a display, copy the number and/or letters on the window display.
6. Complete the Bomb Threat Checklist (reverse side) immediately. Write down as much detail as you can remember. Try to get exact words.
7. Immediately upon termination of the call, do not hang up, but from a different phone, contact FPS immediately with information and await instructions.

If a bomb threat is received by handwritten note:

- Call _____
- Handle note as minimally as possible.

If a bomb threat is received by e-mail:

- Call _____
- Do not delete the message.

Signs of a suspicious package:

- No return address
- Excessive postage
- Stains
- Strange odor
- Strange sounds
- Unexpected Delivery
- Poorly handwritten
- Misspelled Words
- Incorrect Titles
- Foreign Postage
- Restrictive Notes

DO NOT:

- Use two-way radios or cellular phone; radio signals have the potential to detonate a bomb.
- Evacuate the building until police arrive and evaluate the threat.
- Activate the fire alarm.
- Touch or move a suspicious package.

WHO TO CONTACT (select one)

- Follow your local guidelines
- Federal Protective Service (FPS) Police
  1-877-4-FPS-411 (1-877-437-7411)
- 911

BOMB THREAT CHECKLIST

Date:		Time:	
Time Caller Hung Up:		Phone Number where Call Received:	

Ask Caller:

- Where is the bomb located?
  (Building, Floor, Room, etc.)
- When will it go off?
- What does it look like?
- What kind of bomb is it?
- What will make it explode?
- Did you place the bomb?   Yes   No
- Why?
- What is your name?

Exact Words of Threat:

_____
_____
_____
_____
_____

Information About Caller:

- Where is the caller located? (Background and level of noise)
- Estimated age:
- Is voice familiar? If so, who does it sound like?
- Other points:

Caller's Voice	Background Sounds:	Threat Language:
☐ Accent	☐ Animal Noises	☐ Incoherent
☐ Angry	☐ House Noises	☐ Message read
☐ Calm	☐ Kitchen Noises	☐ Taped
☐ Clearing throat	☐ Street Noises	☐ Irrational
☐ Coughing	☐ Booth	☐ Profane
☐ Cracking voice	☐ PA system	☐ Well-spoken
☐ Crying	☐ Conversation	
☐ Deep	☐ Music	
☐ Deep breathing	☐ Motor	
☐ Disguised	☐ Clear	
☐ Distinct	☐ Static	_____
☐ Excited	☐ Office machinery	
☐ Female	☐ Factory machinery	_____
☐ Laughter	☐ Local	
☐ Lisp	☐ Long distance	_____
☐ Loud		
☐ Male	Other Information:	
☐ Nasal		
☐ Normal	_____	
☐ Ragged		
☐ Rapid		
☐ Raspy		
☐ Slow		
☐ Slurred		
☐ Soft		
☐ Stutter		

Workplace Violence and Safety

OSHA (Occupational Safety and Health Administration) defines Workplace Violence as "violence or the threat of violence against workers. It can occur at or outside the workplace and can range from threats and verbal abuse to physical assaults and homicide, one of the leading causes of job-related deaths."

Workplace Violence:

Definition: *Any physical assault, threatening behavior or verbal use (including the use of profanities) in the workplace or setting.*

A workplace or work setting is any place, whether temporary or permanent, where an employee (and volunteers) performs work related duties and responsibilities. A workplace setting can include but is not limited to buildings, campuses, facilities, vehicles, offices, common areas or any place where the employer or organization has supervision and control over.

Nearly 2 million American workers report having been victims of workplace violence each year. Unfortunately, many more cases go unreported. Workplace violence can strike anywhere, anytime, and no one is immune. Among those with higher risk are workers who exchange money with the public, delivery drivers, healthcare professionals, public service workers, customer service agents, law enforcement personnel, and those who work alone or in small groups.

According to Risk Management Magazine, workplace violence cost American businesses and estimated $121 billion in 2002.

"Workplace stress and log hours are creating a growing phenomenon of 'desk rage.' 1 in 10 Americans say they work in an atmosphere where physical violence has occurred because of stress with 42% saying their workplace is a place where yelling and verbal abuse takes place" (Integra Realty Resources).

It is very crucial that employers and administration make clear that workplace violence will absolutely not be tolerated! Notifications must be placed in writing through policies and should also be made through a "campaign" effort such as posters in break rooms or other appropriate areas.

Workplace violence includes:

- ➢ Physical assaults – punching, kicking, scratching, beating, etc.
- ➢ Shootings.
- ➢ Stabbings.
- ➢ Sexual assaults (including attempted)
- ➢ Rapes (including attempted).
- ➢ Harassment and/or intimidation.
- ➢ Shouting.
- ➢ Threats in person, phone, social media, text, device, etc.
- ➢ Being followed or stalked.
- ➢ Suicides.
- ➢ Any behavior that may cause a person to fear for their life.

All of us go to work expecting that we will be able to do our jobs in a safe environment with co-workers and visitors who will be respectful and will keep their composure, even if things don't quite seem to go their way.

Workplace violence came to light during the 1980's and 1990's because of violence within postal facilities. Since then, many employers have addressed this issue by encouraging safety and setting up a formal reporting mechanism. Even with these mechanisms in place, violence does happen and it is important that you take your personal safety into your hands by recognizing signs of possible violence, prevention and response.

Workplace violence acts are committed by strangers, colleagues, family members and personal relations.

Personal Space:

We all have heard at some point or another that we need our space from our parents, colleagues, significant other, etc. Reasons vary but there is always a reason why we make such a request. It's not that we necessarily want to be apart from someone because we dislike them or they did something wrong. Rather asking for a little space is more like a reset button for some. Sometimes being with or working with someone on a daily basis can eventually cause friction or other problems. So, requesting space can be a good thing.

In this chapter, we will go over personal space in more physical terms and why it is so important to your personal safety.

Have you ever entered an elevator and noticed that everyone has their back to the rear of the car or to the sides and no one wants to stand in the middle and face anyone else? There's a good reason for that: they don't want their personal space violated. In other words, it is the area around an individual that others are expected not to enter where we become uncomfortable.

As humans, we all have our personal space boundaries to the front, sides and rear. These boundaries will all depend on who it is you are interacting with. For example, a complete stranger who is visiting with you in your office will most likely not be within a few inches of your face, whereas you may allow close friends and family members to hug or kiss you.

Why is this important?

Simply put: your personal safety!

For the average person, personal space to the front is generally three (3) feet. Once someone has entered that zone, they are now in the intimate zone. Depending on whom you allow to enter your personal space will also determine your level of personal safety.

Let's take an example:

Mr. Smith walks into your office seeking assistance with finding a new property. You know nothing about this person but as a professional you get up from your chair to greet him. He approaches you as you approach him. As a complete stranger (and having read this book) you don't allow him to enter your personal space of three of at least (3) feet. Unbeknownst to you he is armed with a knife.

We can begin to see why keeping your personal space at three feet is so important.

In most situations when interacting with strangers, you will, in taking your personal safety into consideration, give yourself and the other person at minimum four (4) feet or more. That is the minimum number of feet you need to be able to react to a violent situation, whether they are attempting to grab you, punch you, kick you or use a weapon against you. It will also give you the opportunity to escape and call for help.

This individual suddenly brandishes a knife. In keeping your personal space to more four (4) feet, the person has a difficult time reaching you because his striking distance is too far and your reactionary space allows for you to run, hide or fight.

Another way to disengage quickly from the situation is to create a distraction. A distraction may only last a second but may be enough to get away. For example, you can throw a pen, keys, drop papers, etc. It's natural for our eyes to follow the motion – even for that second. It would take another second for the person to realize what happened and react to it. You can also look beyond the person and say something like, "Hey Tom!" The person will naturally look behind them and give you an opportunity to react.

A person seeking to physically harm you will generally look at a specific part of your body first before following through with a blow. Be sure to watch where the person's eyes are targeting.

If you believe a physical assault is imminent, be sure everything you say is loud enough for others to hear. Use commands such as "stop" or "drop the knife (gun, baseball bat, etc.)." Speaking loudly will allow others to call for help or assist you. Ultimately they may become witnesses to what had transpired.

Important: remember not to corner anyone. Feeling cornered may result in more aggressive behavior. Your main goal is the opportunity to escape, rather than engage as a last resort.

I always recommend conducting exercises based on these scenarios so you can get a feel of your reactionary distance. The addition of space between you and the other person will make all the difference in the world – even twelve (12) inches!

Additionally, having someone stand directly beside us, behind us or sitting next to us requires less reactionary space and we are still comfortable with our personal zone.

ACTION WILL USUALLY BEAT REACTION!

Having said all this, it's also important to keep in mind that personal space is relative to:

- ➤ Culture.
- ➤ Impairments.
- ➤ Group dynamics.
- ➤ Geographic location.
- ➤ Our upbringing.
- ➤ Age.
- ➤ Environment.

There are a few signs to look for if you believe someone may become violent:

- ➤ Individual crosses arms tightly.
- ➤ Facial expressions (face turning red, lips tighten and appear to be tense.
- ➤ Point finger directly at you or touching you.
- ➤ Eyebrows drop.
- ➤ Hands on hips.
- ➤ Leaning body to one side.
- ➤ Entering your personal space.
- ➤ Raised voice.

In many cases, individuals commit acts of violence based on past experiences. In this case, the person may have had a not so pleasant experience with a previous Real Estate Agent, perhaps family life is stressful and anger is building, maybe or she just got fired. Whatever the reasons, be aware and look for these signs.

<u>If you are getting mixed messages between verbal and non-verbal – believe the non-verbal messages!!</u>

Domestic Violence:

The U.S. Department of Justice defines Domestic violence as:

"...a pattern of abusive behavior in any relationship that is used by one partner to gain or maintain power and control over another intimate partner. Domestic violence can be physical, sexual, emotional, economic, or psychological actions or threats of actions that influence another person. This includes any behaviors that intimidate, manipulate, humiliate, isolate, frighten, terrorize, coerce, threaten, blame, hurt, injure, or wound someone."

Domestic violence occurs when someone commits to verbal abuse, destroys personal property, harasses or intimidates an intimate partner or other person in order to control another person.

When does it occur?

> ➤ Anytime someone is being overly possessive
> ➤ Deprives person of financial control.
> ➤ Deprives person of physical resources.
> ➤ Family members and close friends are kept away.
> ➤ Physical and verbal abuse.

Anyone can be a victim of domestic violence!

Domestic violence can take place with or without a weapon.

With a weapon, victims can be:

> ➤ Shot.
> ➤ Stabbed.
> ➤ Strangled.
> ➤ Burned.
> ➤ Kicked.
> ➤ Suffocated.
> ➤ Restrained.

Without a weapon, victims can experience:

- ➢ Hair pulling.
- ➢ Biting.
- ➢ Destruction of property.
- ➢ Scratching.
- ➢ Restraining.
- ➢ Grab and hold.
- ➢ Punch.
- ➢ Pinch.
- ➢ Twisting of arms and legs.

Intimidation is generally used as system to control another person. Such acts include displaying weapons, destroying property, throwing things and darting or glaring stares.

Emotionally, partners call each other names, put each other down, they make the other partner feel bad about themselves or make them think they are going crazy.

Domestic violence has a tendency to spillover into the work place. While we make every attempt to keep our personal lives private, sometimes it doesn't quite work out that way. Your partner may harass you at work via telephone or present him/herself at your job. You should immediately alert security staff or receptionist (if available) that you are not available for their calls or visits. Immediately contact law enforcement, particularly if the partner has a court issued restraining order placed on them, if you are being threatened or you believe you are in imminent danger.

Bullying:

No one deserves to be bullied-period!

The Workplace Bullying Institute defines "bullying" as repeated, health-harming mistreatment of one or more persons (the targets) by one or more perpetrators. It is *abusive conduct* that is threatening, humiliating, or intimidating, work interference, sabotage — which prevents work from getting done, or verbal abuse."

We don't often hear about bullying in the workplace and many times it goes unreported or underreported. Some employees may believe they will be demoted, fired or further harassed if they say something. Many employees believe that bullying is part of the workplace culture perhaps because it's natural to be competitive in the office.

Bullying in the workplace is slightly different than bullying in a school in that children who are bullied at school are targeted because they have no friends, appear to be strange, different or weak and often do not fight back. Acts of bullying are committed by those who are physically strong and have the ability of enticing others to join them in committing such acts.

In the workplace, bullies tend to be those individuals who they perceive to be a threat. Individuals who are on the receiving end of these behaviors are often employees who have worked at the company for many years and are more experienced than some of their colleagues. In general, others seek their guidance and opinions on work related matters. Additionally superiors or other colleagues who are insecure about their position or abilities tend to discredit or sabotage others through harassing behaviors directly and indirectly and will often make every effort to take credit to make themselves look good.

The bullied, often called "targets," tend to be honest, ethical and possess integrity. They are generally well liked by other co-workers and customers alike. They will possess maturity, have the ability to think things through and be able to reason. In addition, they are caring, are willing to help others and will show warmth and empathy.

The targets are generally non-confrontational to their bullies but are not submissive and do not return the aggression which makes the bully's intimidation even more harsh at times. The bully will carry on their behavior if the employer makes no attempt to intervene or stop such actions and the target does not report it.

Unfortunately Human Resources and chief executives have a difficult time in containing or stopping this. From their perspective, the bully could be a star performer they need or more importantly do not want to become confrontational. In worst case scenarios orders to bully an employee can come right from the top for retaliation of any action the employee may have taken in the past.

For some, bullying can cause depression and other health and mental health related issues.

Documentation:

If you believe that workplace bullying is taking place, begin to document it. You should include date, time, by whom, what was said and the action you took at the time. Be sure to also note any superiors you may have spoken to. Ideally you will want to get written statement s from co-workers as part of your documentation package. However, don't be surprised if they are less than willing to help you because they may fear retaliation or job loss. If your company employs security professionals, be sure to report it to them along with your documentation and statements. Give them copies of your paperwork-always maintain the originals! Follow up with the officer assigned to take your report and request a copy of a written report when available. Note that some security departments, as a matter of policy, will maintain any reports generated as confidential and may not be released to you without authorization from legal counsel or other representative. If this is pursued in a court of law, your attorney can try to subpoena them.

Audio recording conversations or statements can present its own set of legal challenges. For example, Connecticut requires consent of all parties to a conversation. Regardless of the number of people in that conversation, you must receive each person's consent and you must be a party to the conversation.

Always seek the advice of an attorney.

"By acquiring knowledge you are investing in yourself."

Dan Sinisi

Terrorism

Title 22 of the U.S. Code, Section 2656f(d) defines terrorism as "premeditated, politically motivated violence perpetrated against noncombatant targets by subnational groups or clandestine agents, usually intended to influence an audience."

The Federal Bureau of Investigation (FBI) defines terrorism as "the unlawful use of force or violence against persons or property to intimidate or coerce a government, the civilian population, or any segment thereof, in furtherance of political or social objectives."

While the U.S. Department of Homeland Security (DHS), The FBI, the State Department, state and local agencies make every attempt to keep the United States and its' citizens free form terrorism, Private Security Officers also play a vital role in securing our nation. There are numerous landmarks and properties that are secured by private security. Security Officers must be ever vigilant of suspicious persons, vehicles, packages, trespassers, etc.

Of particular interest are persons who are photographing the property, asking about the security program, or appear too friendly. While these behaviors may be innocent and they are not breaking any laws or violating rules, if you believe they are suspicious, make notes and be as detailed as possible. Do not take anything for granted! They could be potential terrorists "scouting" and gathering information. If a terrorist act does occur, you can refer back to your notes as law enforcement begin to investigate.

Everyone is responsible for their own safety!

Types of Terrorism:

Cyber-terrorism: Cyber-terrorists use information technology to attack civilians and draw attention to their cause. This may mean that they use information technology, such as computer systems or telecommunications, as a tool to orchestrate a traditional attack. More often, cyber-terrorism refers to an attack on information technology itself in a way that would radically disrupt networked services. For example, cyber-terrorists could disable networked emergency systems or hack into networks housing critical financial information.

Eco-terrorism: Eco-Terrorism is a political terrorism using sabotage, arson and violence in order to achieve environmentalist aims.

Domestic Terrorism: Means activities with the following three characteristics:

➤ Involve acts dangerous to human life that violate federal or state law;
➤ Appear intended (i) to intimidate or coerce a civilian population; (ii) to influence the policy of a government by intimidation or coercion; or (iii) to affect the conduct of a government by mass destruction, assassination. or kidnapping; and
➤ Occur primarily within the territorial jurisdiction of the U.S.

International Terrorism: Means activities with the following three characteristics:

➤ Involve violent acts or acts dangerous to human life that violate federal or state law;
➤ Appear to be intended (i) to intimidate or coerce a civilian population; (ii) to influence the policy of a government by intimidation or coercion; or (iii) to affect the conduct of a government by mass destruction, assassination, or kidnapping; and
➤ Occur primarily outside the territorial jurisdiction of the U.S., or transcend national boundaries in terms of the means by which they are accomplished, the persons they appear intended to intimidate or coerce, or the locale in which their perpetrators operate or seek asylum.

Bio-Terrorism: Refers to the intentional release of toxic biological agents to harm and terrorize civilians, in the name of a political or other cause.

Responding to a Terrorist Act:

As an employee you may find yourself to be the first responder. Those responding to terrorist incidents must be aware of the extreme dangers associated with these types of disasters. It is important to recognize that any disaster could be a terrorist attack. There are others things to consider when responding to the scene of a terrorist attack. The incident scene may be extremely dangerous and it is also a crime scene.

Before rushing in, look for identifiers of Weapons of Mass Destruction (WMDs):
➢ Biological
➢ Nuclear
➢ Incendiary
➢ Chemical
➢ Explosive

The scene may include secondary devices (bombs designed to take out emergency responders). In order to respond effectively to terrorist scenes, you should be extremely cautious. Responders should be aware at all times of the circumstances in which they find themselves. A particular concern is to ensure the scene is as secure as possible.

➢ All personnel entering the site should have identification and a justified reason for being there.
➢ Incident commanders may need to refuse donations if they appear suspicious.
➢ Fences and barricades may be needed to keep citizens out of the area.
➢ Scanning the area on ground to detect further potentially harmful terrorist activities.

Active Shooter

In recent years, active shooter incidents appear to have increased in number and intensity. Unfortunately it's difficult to determine when one will occur or by whom. It seems no place is immune from these acts of violence. Schools, hospitals, churches, businesses, malls and other public and private properties are no longer considered sanctuaries. Persons who become dissatisfied with society, government, employers or life in general may consider violence as an outlet to their feelings. Many believe they are getting a "raw deal" or they have been convinced they are superior. In recent years, some active shooters have become "radicalized" and believe they must resort to violence in order to prove their religious faith.

The United States Department of Homeland Security defines "active shooter" as "an individual actively engaged in killing or attempting to kill people in a confined or populated area."

According to the U.S. Department of Justice, there are <u>five phases</u> of an active shooter. You should keep these in mind if developing a policy and interacting with others:

Fantasy Stage:

> ➤ Individual(s) dreams of shooting.
> ➤ Seeking media attention and glory.
> ➤ Seeks in breaking the death count from previous active shooters.
> ➤ Wants to go out in a blaze of glory.

Planning Stage:

> ➤ Determines logistics.
> ➤ Discusses plans with others.
> ➤ May put plans down on paper or social media.
> ➤ The time and location are decided.
> ➤ Target specific people.

Preparation Stage:

> ➤ Obtain explosives, bomb making materials and weapons.
> ➤ Conduct a practice or walk-through of the operation.
> ➤ Call others and advise not to go into work, school, etc.

Approach Stage:

> ➤ Committed to carrying out the act.

Implementation Stage:

> ➤ Law enforcement officers need to stop the threat.
> ➤ Active shooter will continue to shoot.
> ➤ Civilians may have to use any force including deadly force to neutralize the shooter.

Responding to an Active Shooter Event:

> Active shooter situations are unpredictable and can take place anywhere at any time.
> In most cases, active shooters use firearms and there is no pattern of selection of victims.
> Usually active shooter situations are over in ten (10) to fifteen (15) minutes.
> Immediate law enforcement response is needed to stop or mitigate the shooting.
> According to the U.S. Department of Homeland Security and the Federal Bureau of Investigation, citizens will have to intervene until law enforcement arrival.
> Be proactive in your response.
> After being notified there is a person with a gun immediately find cover and dial 911.
> Once you are in a secure location or cover, conduct a *scene size-up - identify threat and assess the situation.
> From a safe location, observe the situation from a distance and if safe to do so take action or if possible relay information safely to others without giving away your position!

You can survive an active shooter event! The key is to remain as calm as possible. If others are panicking, try to assure them and work together as a team.

If you find yourself in a violent situation, you must take immediate, decisive and committed action!

Options:

RUN:

> If there is a path available and there is an escape route, attempt to evacuate!
> Do not hesitate – leave immediately!
> Leave your belongings behind – your life is the most important matter!
> Evacuate whether others agree or not – there is no time debate!
> If possible, help others escape!
> Once out of the area of danger, be sure to exit with your hands in the air! Arriving law enforcement will not immediately know who the shooter is!
> Give arriving emergency responders as much information about the situation including a description of the shooter, location, how many people may still be in the area, etc.
> There is a very good chance you will be debriefed by investigators or other officials. Do not speak or accept interviews with the media. The scene could still be active and the number one priority is your safety!

HIDE:

- ➢ If you are unable to leave safely, hide, find cover or shelter yourself as best you can!
- ➢ Lay low and stay out of shooter's view!
- ➢ Silence your phone and do not draw attention to yourself!
- ➢ Lock all doors and barricade yourself!
- ➢ Call 911 if it is safe to do so!
- ➢ Have a plan – <u>assess the situation</u> – will you run, continue to hide or fight?
- ➢ Do your best to remain calm – continually assess the situation!
- ➢ Be prepared to fight if necessary!

FIGHT:

➤ <u>Physical action should be employed as a last resort!</u>
➤ You may have no choice but to fight!
➤ Fight or engage with complete commitment!
➤ Be physically aggressive!
➤ Deadly use of force may be necessary!
➤ Use improvised weapons - **anything can be used as a weapon!**
➤ Fight or engage to incapacitate, stop and neutralize the shooter!

If the threat has been neutralized (i.e. shooter is injured, killed or taken into custody), you should exit the facility with hands up in the air. Until the scene is neutralized and the all clear is given, law enforcement can't differentiate possible shooters from innocent civilians. You are more at risk when exiting as the shooter may have changed clothes with you. Law enforcement has to confirm your identity and be absolutely sure you are not the shooter!

Active shooters will generally commit acts of violence on "soft targets." These targets are considered to be people or places that are relatively unprotected or vulnerable.

Legal Powers and Responsibilities

Before and even after the founding of our country, all able-bodied men were required to assist with the apprehension of criminals. Today with the advent of professional police forces and private security, many of us will unlikely be arresting or detaining anyone for various reasons. However, as a citizen, you should be informed and have knowledge in this area if you choose to pursue this.

Unless you are a "commissioned" Officer, in most jurisdictions private citizens have only the power of a private citizen - generally referred to as "citizen's arrest."

Detention and Arrest:

In most states, private citizens are allowed to detain a person they "reasonably" believe has committed a crime. However, the Courts have also ruled that you make an arrest every time you stop someone and you do not allow the person to leave freely or the person feels they are not free to leave.

If you have no reason or you have a "reasonable belief" that a crime was committed and you stop and detain an individual, you are actually arresting that person, even if the person is not handcuffed or restrained. The private citizen may face civil litigation and/or could be charged with false imprisonment.

The standard of "reasonable belief" means that the average person in the same circumstances would have the same belief and take the same actions.

In most cases when a person is being detained, it is almost always on a voluntary basis unless said person is held in a back office, security room, a vehicle, or in handcuffs.

Private citizens can only detain someone for a reasonable amount of time. Additionally, you can detain a person who is on the property unlawfully or is suspicious. If you detain an individual, be sure to take your safety into consideration by doing it reasonably, safely and being aware of your surroundings. If possible, have someone witness the detention.

Unlike law enforcement officers, private citizens do not have to give Miranda warnings to the person.

<u>Remember – as the property owner or as an agent for your employer, you have the right to stop and question anyone at anytime on private property!</u>

- Generally, the individual should not be held in detention or custody for more than 30-60 minutes prior to contacting law enforcement.
- Stay in public areas (i.e. hallways, parking lots, etc.).
- In an office or other room, keep the door open.
- Record the interview if possible and permitted.
- Immediately notify law enforcement if the person is under arrest.
- Do not allow the individual to smoke as it can cause a fire, disruption or can be used as a weapon against you.
- Do not allow the person to consume food or drink as this can give that person a closer contact and greater ability to assault you.

<u>Citizen's Arrest Standard:</u>

All states permit "citizen's arrest" so long as a felony crime is witnessed by the citizen making the arrest or when a citizen is asked by law enforcement to assist in apprehending a suspect. Laws vary by state with regards to misdemeanor crime, beaches of the peace and felonies not witnessed by the arresting citizen.

Things to keep in mind if making an arrest:

- The person you are attempting to arrest may be armed and dangerous.
- There is a good chance the arrestee will resist and therefore you may be injured or killed.
- The citizen may not be properly trained or equipped to handle such arrests.

Additionally:

- Citizens must only use the amount of force that is reasonable and necessary to make the arrest.
- The citizen making the arrest may only use deadly physical force when faced with the threat of serious bodily harm and/or to prevent harm to themselves or others.
- Excessive force may result in criminal charges against the arresting citizen
- The arresting citizen could expose themselves to civil liability and lawsuits.
- Possible charges of impersonating a Police Officer, false imprisonment, kidnapping or wrongful arrest could result.

Use of Force

For those of us not directly involved in the public safety profession, it is proper and fitting that we briefly cover a citizen's ability to use force to protect themselves, others, and property. However, as stated earlier, the chances that real estate professionals will involve themselves in a use of force incident is minimal at best.

In Connecticut, the following statutes exist:

53a-19 – Use of Physical Force in Defense of Person:

*"**(a)** Except as provided in subsections (b) and (c) of this section, a person is justified in using reasonable physical force upon another person to defend himself or a third person from what he reasonably believes to be the use or imminent use of physical force, and he may use such degree of force which he reasonably believes to be necessary for such purpose; except that deadly physical force may not be used unless the actor reasonably believes that such other person is:*
(1) using or about to use deadly physical force, or
(2) inflicting or about to inflict great bodily harm."

*"**(b)** Notwithstanding the provisions of subsection (a) of this section, a person is not justified in using deadly physical force upon another person if he or she knows that he or she can avoid the necessity of using such force with complete safety:*
(1) by retreating, except that the actor shall not be required to retreat if he or she is in his or her dwelling, as defined in section 53a-100, or place of work and was not the initial aggressor, or if he or she is a peace officer, a special policeman appointed under section 29-18b, or a motor vehicle inspector designated under section 14-8 and certified pursuant to section 7-294d, or a private person assisting such peace officer, special policeman or motor vehicle inspector at his or her direction, and acting pursuant to section 53a-22, or
(2) by surrendering possession of property to a person asserting a claim of right thereto, or
"(3) by complying with a demand that he or she abstain from performing an act which he or she is not obliged to perform.

(c) Notwithstanding the provisions of subsection (a) of this section, a person is not justified in using physical force when:

(1) with intent to cause physical injury or death to another person, he provokes the use of physical force by such other person, or

(2) he is the initial aggressor, except that his use of physical force upon another person under such circumstances is justifiable if he withdraws from the encounter and effectively communicates to such other person his intent to do so, but such other person notwithstanding continues or threatens the use of physical force, or

(3) the physical force involved was the product of a combat by agreement not specifically authorized by law."

53a-20 – Use of Physical Force in Defense of Premises:

"A person in possession or control of premises, or a person who is licensed or privileged to be in or upon such premises, is justified in using reasonable physical force upon another person when and to the extent that he reasonably believes such to be necessary to prevent or terminate the commission or attempted commission of a criminal trespass by such other person in or upon such premises; but he may use deadly physical force under such circumstances only:

(1) in defense of a person as prescribed in section 53a-19, or

(2) when he reasonably believes such to be necessary to prevent an attempt by the trespasser to commit arson or any crime of violence, or

(3) to the extent that he reasonably believes such to be necessary to prevent or terminate an unlawful entry by force into his dwelling as defined in section 53a-100, or place of work, and for the sole purpose of such prevention or termination."

53a-21 – Use of Physical Force in Defense of Property:

"A person is justified in using reasonable physical force upon another person when and to the extent that he reasonably believes such to be necessary to prevent an attempt by such other person to commit larceny or criminal mischief involving property, or when and to the extent he reasonably believes such to be necessary to regain property which he reasonably believes to have been acquired by larceny within a reasonable time prior to the use of such force; but he may use deadly physical force under such circumstances only in defense of person as prescribed in section 53a-19."

Private Citizens enjoy no special "Use of Force Rights" as their Law Enforcement counterparts!!

It's very important that you familiarize yourself with your employer's policies and state statutes concerning the use of force should you have to employ it. In many circumstances, the best way to deal with a situation is to be a good witness. Don't be a hero! We all want to go home to our families!

To put this in perspective, we have to appreciate law enforcement's standard in the implementation of the use of force. Keep in mind the continuum does not apply to private citizens (outside of security professionals). Rather, I am making comparisons so there is an understanding of when and how certain levels of force are reached.

Law Enforcement Use of Force Continuum:

Officer's presence in uniform:

> ➢ Highly visible as a deterrent to crime.
> ➢ Officer's attitudes and demeanor are professional and non-threatening.

Verbalization – force is not physical:

> ➢ Officers issue calm, nonthreatening commands, such as "Let me see your identification and registration."
> ➢ Officers may increase their volume and shorten commands in an attempt to gain compliance. Short commands might include "Stop," or "Don't move."

Empty hand control:

> ➢ Officer uses bodily force to gain control of a situation.
> ➢ *Soft technique:* Officers use grabs, holds and joint locks to restrain an individual.
> ➢ *Hard technique:* Officers use punches and kicks to restrain an individual.

Less than lethal:

> Officers use less than lethal technologies to gain control of a situation.
> *Blunt impact.* Officers may use a baton or projectile to immobilize a combative person.
> *Chemical.* Officers may use chemical sprays or projectiles embedded with chemicals to restrain an individual (e.g., pepper spray).
> *Conducted Energy Devices (CEDs).* Officers may use CEDs to immobilize an individual. CEDs discharge a high-voltage, low-amperage jolt of electricity at a distance (i.e. Tasers).

Lethal force:

> **Officers use lethal weapons to gain control of a situation. Should only be used if a suspect poses a serious threat to the officer or another individual.**
> Officers use deadly weapons such as firearms to stop an individual's actions.

YOU SHOULD ONLY USE LETHAL FORCE WHEN ALL OTHER ALTERNATIVES HAVE BEEN EXHAUSTED!

You should consider the following when employing any level of force:
> Be aware of your surroundings. Is there anyone else in the background who might assault you?
> Are you able to safely retreat and call for assistance?
> If you are able to retreat, will others be in danger?
> Is there somewhere to retreat to?
> If need be, are you able to engage the person?

Whether you are indoors or outdoors, *anything* can be used as a weapon to defend yourself if you believe you are in imminent danger – but always remember the same applies to your assailant – be prepared and be aware of your surroundings at all times!!

Safety in the Field

Be aware of your surroundings! I can't stress this enough. There is so much going on around us that most of the time we take things for granted. Whether you live in an urban city or suburban town your personal safety must always be a priority.

Always inform your office of where you will be, who you will be with and when you will next be in touch. Make sure the person you are meeting knows that you've given your office this information.

Many professionals create profiles on their social media platforms, websites and business cards. Here are a few things to keep in mind in keeping yourself safe:

- Do not display expensive jewelry in your profile or in the field. This could easily make you a potential target people posing as clients.
- Do not give out your home address.
- The background in your photo should not display family members or give away where you live.
- Do not give out your home phone number.
- Keep your personal social media pages on privacy or restricted settings.

On the Road:

Like many other professionals, our personal vehicles can sometimes be our mobile office. For this reason, it's important that you think of your vehicle as your "castle." Be sure the vehicle is well maintained, has all appropriate inspections, is serviced regularly and everything inside and outside the vehicle works properly before departing to your destination. The last thing you need is for the vehicle to break down because of something avoidable.

Keep your windows rolled up and the doors locked each and every time you step away from your vehicle, even if it's just briefly. Many people believe having the vehicle parked at work or in their own driveway makes it less likely the vehicle will be stolen or items taken. This is not always the case. Criminals will always look for an easy opportunity regardless where the vehicle is parked. Be sure to arm the alarm system if applicable. Keep in mind you may have sensitive data including your personal information as to where you live and work. Protect your client's information as well as yours.

Where you park your vehicle is also important, especially at night. If possible, park under or in the vicinity of a street light. By doing this, your vehicle will be lit and anyone attempting to break into the vehicle will have potential witnesses. Many criminals prefer to commit their crimes under the cover of dark because there is less likelihood they will be seen and will have an easier time escaping unnoticed. Do not keep anything in plain view. It's just an invitation to have your vehicle broken into.

Most of us take the same route to work, to the gym or even a friend's house because we become accustomed to where we are and how to get there. Sometimes we don't want to take other roads or highways for fear of getting lost or maybe it's an inconvenience. As a volunteer Fire/Police Officer, I like to give this analogy to participants in our training that best explains this:

"One evening our station was toned out for a serious motor vehicle accident on a local road. Upon arrival, the chief immediately assigned me to respond to the nearest intersection to direct traffic away from the scene. Shortly thereafter, a motorist approached and asked to be let through even though the person didn't live in the area. The driver was advised to take an alternative route after explaining how to get around. The driver said for twenty years she had taken the same route home to a nearby town. With so much going on and other vehicles behind her, I simply stated that she would be learning a new route that night."

While my answer was direct and appears to be non-supportive, it was a reality check for that driver. The lesson here is that you should always know more than one way to get to your destination. Criminals do their homework. If they find a target, they will watch everything you do and everywhere you go. They will note the times you are away from your vehicle or your home. It's your job to make their job more difficult by being unpredictable. They may plan on committing their crime at a particular traffic light you always stop at, a drive- thru or they may feign vehicle trouble and force you to slow down or stop. Don't give them the opportunity to plan when and where. You're best offense is a good defense, that being to keep them guessing.

As stated earlier, we tend to use our vehicles as offices. We sometimes find ourselves distracted, thinking about our next presentation or perhaps what to make for dinner. Driving is a full time job and requires you to be alert. Once you place yourself behind the wheel, your senses should take over. Don't allow conversations with others or phone calls/texts distract you from being able to appropriately respond to any given situation. Your focus should be on the road in front of you while scanning left to right. The author has witnessed on many occasions drivers drinking their coffee, putting on makeup and even reading, all while driving. The chances of hurting yourself or others go up dramatically. According to the National Highway Traffic Safety Administration, nearly 3,500 people or 0.82 deaths per 100,000 occurred in accidents involving distracted driving. Connecticut law prohibits the use of cell phones while driving. If you must call or text, pull over and park your vehicle in a safe place. Be sure you are mindful of your surroundings at all times. Also keep the noise level in the car down to a minimum. Blasting the radio or any device will certainly get you the wrong attention and it will become more difficult to use your sense of hearing.

The Governors Highway Safety Association states that Connecticut is not alone in the rise of pedestrian fatalities. While the state is lower than the national average, take into consideration that distracted driving takes away your ability to make split second decisions and your reactionary time.

Driving under the influence of alcohol or drugs is also a distraction. You're ability to function as a driver become impaired and could cause you many legal headaches let alone the possibility of injuring or killing yourself or others.

Carjacking:

We would all like to think that we are safe in our vehicles. Unfortunately crimes are committed that involve you, the vehicle or both. Sometimes these are crimes of opportunity. Many vehicles on the road today are equipped with state of the art alarms systems and locks, thus discouraging some criminals from making any attempt into breaking in while the vehicle is parked. However, this makes carjacking a more reasonable alternative because of the ease in committing this crime. It provides criminals with several reasons why it's committed in the first place:

> The make and model of the car are in high demand. Parts for certain vehicles on the black market can fetch large sums of money and are sometimes shipped to foreign countries.
> Committing a crime then using the vehicle as a "get a way car." Sometimes the vehicle carjacked will be used in other crimes and then abandoned.
> Committing a violent crime against the driver and/or passengers such as kidnapping, rape, robbery or murder.

Criminals will always look for the easiest "mark" such as the elderly, females that are driving alone or with children and drivers who are not paying attention and are not aware of their surroundings. Parking in an isolated or dark are is also an invite for criminals.

Carjacking Prevention and How to Protect Yourself:

- ➤ Park in a well lit area and near other vehicles.
- ➤ As you approach your parked vehicle, look around you and be aware of your surroundings. Do not become distracted by phone or personal conversations.
- ➤ Have your keys in your hand before reaching the vehicle. Looking for your keys in your purse or pocket at the vehicle will give a potential criminal the advantage and take you by surprise.
- ➤ Have a flashlight handy to help light the way. There are various sizes and illumination types on the market to fit on a keychain or in a purse/pocket.
- ➤ Most keys have fobs attached that allow you to lock/unlock the vehicle. They also include a panic button that will activate the car alarm. If you feel threatened, press the panic button to get attention. In most cases, this will drive a potential criminal away.
- ➤ If approached by someone whom you feel threatened and appears to be unarmed, use a distraction technique. For example throw your keys, books, pens, etc away. The criminal will naturally look away at the direction of what you threw which will give you a second or two to react or escape. You can also shout someone's name i.e. "Hey Joe!" and point anywhere. Do the same as above.

"Look all around you for this will help you in your travels."

Dan Sinisi

<u>While Driving:</u>

- ➢ Be aware of your surroundings! Pay attention to where you are. Do your best to look confident and not distracted.
- ➢ Keep vehicle doors locked at all times and windows rolled up at all times regardless of temperature or weather conditions. The vehicle's air conditioner/fan and heating system should solve any concern about getting air.
- ➢ If possible, avoid driving alone, especially at night and in unfamiliar areas. Have a GPS or map readily available in case you get lost. If you are going to stop and ask for directions be sure you are in a well lit area with other people around.
- ➢ If you see a person with vehicle trouble on the side of the road, do not stop. It could be a diversion to get you out of your vehicle. Call law enforcement for assistance.
- ➢ Lock your vehicle at all times, even if you are stepping away momentarily. Things can happen in an instant.
- ➢ Consistently scan your surroundings! Carjackings often take place when you are stopped at a traffic light, stop sign or any other time you are not moving.
- ➢ Keep all your valuables under the seats or in the trunk.

There are many ways in which a criminal may take your car while an incident appears to be legitimate. For instance, you feel a light tap on your rear bumper. The natural thing for us to do is to pull over, look at the damage and exchange insurance information with the other driver. That's exactly what carjackers want you to do. Usually these criminals work in pairs. While you are distracted by the other driver the passenger will jump into your vehicle and take off or may rob and/or assault you. If you should be "tapped" from behind, look in your rearview and side mirrors to see if the driver and or passengers appear to be suspicious. Always go with your "gut feeling." If something just doesn't feel right, keep driving and do not pull over until you have reached a populated area or a well lit area with people. Population areas will contain possible witnesses should something occur. If there are no areas that work for you, a police station, fire station or municipal/public building will work also. Of course if you see a fire truck or patrol car you can stop there too. Signal to the other vehicle to follow you while observing their movements in the mirrors. If they fail to pull over at the location you have chosen, try to take their vehicle information down such as license plate marker, make and model, color and if possible descriptions of the vehicle occupants. You should also note the direction of travel to pass on to law enforcement.

In another method, the vehicle in front of you will suddenly slow down or come to a complete stop usually in slow moving traffic. You then accidentally hit them from behind. The same scenario above plays out only there may be an additional vehicle that stops right behind you without you noticing because you are "exchanging" information with the driver in front of you. If this type of incident occurs, immediately call law enforcement or 911. It's imperative that you are always alert and know what's going on.

Response to a Carjacking:

Reacting to a carjacking can pose numerous dilemmas for you. Do you fight or resist? There are many variables in the outcome of these situations and different consequences. Each person is unique in how they will choose to respond. The most important thing to remember is to value your life above everything else. Your vehicle and any objects can be replaced but not your life.

If you are confronted by someone with a weapon i.e. firearm, knife, club, etc. give up your vehicle keys and get away from the area and immediately notify law enforcement. An angry or agitated criminal has the potential to become very violent and they themselves become the weapon. If you are in the vehicle, exit immediately and leave everything behind! In the process make every possible effort to get any description of the criminal(s) and any other pertinent information. Should children be present in the vehicle, shout out loud that you have a child. If applicable unbuckle the restraint while saying in a loud voice that you have a child(ren). By shouting you will get attention from nearby people to assist you or at the very least be witnesses. Remove the child and leave immediately.

If you are kidnapped and are placed into the trunk-remain calm! Locate and kick out the tail lights if possible. If successful, this will give you the opportunity to stick your arm out and draw attention. Having a small flashlight in this instance would be beneficial. Regardless, you can feel for the tail lights.

If you are placed in front passenger or rear seats and you believe you are imminent danger they are several options:

➤ You can attempt to jump out of the vehicle. In order to do this the vehicle must be moving slowing enough where the chances of great bodily harm are diminished significantly and the driver is distracted. Choose a soft landing location such as a grassy area if possible. Leave the area immediately and seek help. Attempt this only if these criteria are met.

➢ Grab the steering the wheel and direct the vehicle into parked cars. In this option, there is a good chance someone will report the erratic driving. Do not attempt this in a high speed vehicle.

➢ Anything can be used as a weapon. Whatever objects are in the vehicle can be used to distract, injure or as a last resort kill the carjacker.

➢ If the criminal is holding a handgun and is pointing it at you grab the gun by the muzzle and point it away from you. Attempt to disarm the criminal. <u>This should only be attempted in extreme imminent danger!</u>

<u>Meeting With Clients:</u>

Real Estate professionals spend a lot time meeting with clients as part of the property buying process. However, unless you know the client well from past experience, chances are you will have to take extra steps to ensure your safety. Do not meet anyone solely based on a phone call. Have the potential client meet you in the office first to ascertain if this is legitimate business.

First, when making an appointment with your client to preview a property, ask a trusted colleague to come with you. There is strength in numbers. The author strongly recommends you do a "dry run" of not only the property but the route you will be taking to get there as discussed earlier. Become familiar with the area and take note of the neighborhood for unusual activity. Inside the structure, look for possible escape doors and make metal notes of anything that can be used as a weapon i.e. kitchen knives, tools, household chemicals, etc. Being prepared ahead of time will give you a greater advantage.

Prior to departing, be sure to let someone know where you are going, whom you are meeting with and approximately how long you will be there. Your cell phone should be full charged and readily available. It's always a good idea to have a phrase or safety word that only you and the office know about so that if you feel threatened you can let your colleague or office via phone call and trigger an appropriate response.

Have the client meet you at the property to be visited. It's strongly recommended that you and the client arrive in separate vehicles. Remember, your vehicle is your "castle" and you will have greater control and safety in your vehicle while driving. You don't want to be surprised by the client you just picked up brandishing a weapon or strong-arming you to drive to an unknown location with less than good intentions.

Once you arrive, let the client enter the property first. By doing this, you will be keeping your personal space intact and you won't have someone behind. Ideally you should have the client in front of you at all times throughout the property and always at a safe distance so you have the time to react should you need it. Be sure all exterior doors are unlocked in the event you need to make a quick escape. Continue to scan your surroundings. Don't allow yourself to be cornered. Place yourself in or at the doorway of any room.

Upon completion of your preview meeting, escort the client back out the door of the property. Remain at the doorway until your client leaves. Do a walk- through of the property from top to bottom and front to back locking the doors behind you to be sure there are no surprises. Remember to be aware of your surroundings!

These same precautions also apply to open houses. The listing real estate professional should have everyone sign a logbook to include vehicle information. This is an excellent record should something be stolen or other crime committed and is a valuable starting point should law enforcement conduct an investigation.

The author recommends that previews take place during regular business hours. If you plan to preview with a client in the evening or "after hours" times definitely bring along a trusted person to support you should something occur. Dressing professionally also lets the client know this is a business meeting and to keep things professional.

Company "For Sale" signs posted on the property are standard practice. However, you may wish to consider only placing your first initial and last name to conceal your gender and prevent anyone unknown to you from asking for you by name. If possible no name placement other than the company would be ideal.

There are many professionals who meet clients outside the workplace to conduct business. This type of meeting offers a more relaxed setting in which to discuss business but also provides ample opportunity to become vulnerable and distracted thus placing your personal safety at risk. If you must conduct business in a casual setting, insist on meeting in a public area. There must be a balance between wooing the client and your safety.

As stated previously, meet the client at the location. Never pick them up or be picked up. You want complete control from departure to return. By doing this you will have the advantage of leaving at anytime, especially if the meeting appears to be going in a direction that you feel uncomfortable with. Dress the part of the professional and let others know where you will be and with whom. Have your cell phone fully charged and readily available.

Every effort should be made to not meet at the client's residence if at all possible. You will not have the advantage of being familiar with the house and there are too many unknowns before even stepping in the door. Meet in public-it's your best bet. If you must do so, apply the principles outlined in this chapter.

Many business meetings take place in establishments that serve alcohol. If you must meet in a place like this remember that alcoholic beverages lowers your inhibitions. You should ask the server to sit you in a well lit area preferably near other people. Be sure your back is facing the wall so you can get a better view of what's around you and the door. Scan the establishment for emergency exits should an incident occur so you can quickly leave and have a plan should things not go well. The author also recommends scanning the people around you to see who may be able to assist you if you have a problem and need assistance.

If a client offers to buy you a drink, you should politely decline and ask for a non-alcoholic beverage. Consuming alcohol may impair your judgment both personal and professional. Once your beverage is served, keep a close eye on it to make sure certain that no one, including your client, can slip drugs or other things into your drink. Should you decide to consume alcohol, space your drinks with plenty of water so you will be able to still remain vigilant. Also keep a watchful eye on your client if they are consuming alcohol and the number of drinks they order. If they begin to slur their speech and appear to be intoxicated, this would be a good time to end the engagement and leave. Under no circumstances should you offer a ride back to the client's residence, even with the best of intentions. Calling the client a taxi or friend for them would be in your best interest. Don't put yourself in a vulnerable position.

Be sure to keep the meeting in a professional tone. Sometimes we start off with "small talk" before jumping in to our reason for getting together. Make every effort to divulge as little personal information as possible. Be non-specific about places you and your friends like to hang out, restaurants you frequent, etc. Don't give anyone a reason to stalk you particularly if they know your routines or where you might be.

Business meetings should not include children if at all possible, particularly in an unfamiliar location. Understandably, sometimes there is no other choice. Bring another person with you who can watch over them so you are not distracted and your children will be safe.

Politics will often play into any conversation with everyone having an opinion. Remember that politics may also lead to contentious conversations which can turn into an emotionally charged discussion. The political climate has the ability to bring out emotions ranging from depressed to angry and perhaps violent. Remain neutral and pick another topic.

Emergency Communications and 911:

In the United States, almost every jurisdiction employs the Emergency 911 system. Simply put, you can pick up any phone and by dialing 911, you will immediately be connected to an emergency Tele-Communicator or as they are more commonly known as emergency dispatchers.

Dispatchers have years of experience with many having served as law enforcement officers, firefighters and Paramedics. Dispatchers can come in the form of sworn personnel or civilians. Either way, both are highly trained, knowledgeable and deal with many diverse situations. Emergency communication centers boast state of the art digitized equipment including maps, nearest emergency vehicles and other information that would be helpful in an emergency such as guiding a caller through CPR for example.

With many of us using cell phones these days, it's important to note that dialing 911 does not necessarily mean that a dispatcher from your hometown will pick up especially if you are mobile. There's a good chance the state police may respond to your call and if necessary re-direct the call to the jurisdiction you happen to be in.

Keep in mind that with all the state of the art equipment at their disposal, dispatchers will still need information from you to determine which assets (i.e. police, fire, EMS, etc.) to deploy to your location. It's important that you remain as calm as possible when speaking to a dispatcher. Speak clearly and don't allow other distractions to hamper you from providing valuable information. Depending on your circumstances, dispatchers may ask you a series of questions including what happened, condition of a person, description of persons, etc. The dispatcher may request that you remain on the line to be sure you're safe until emergency responders arrive. You are the eyes and the ears of the dispatcher while on the line.

Customer Care and Interaction

In all service industries, customer care is always on the top of the list in how responsibilities are performed. Almost all companies, large and small, make taking care of the customer (i.e. client, employees, visitors, vendors, etc.) a top priority. In fact, public safety agencies across the country and around the world are taking a page from the private sector to improve public relations. Many law enforcement patrol vehicles have written "protect and serve" and "to serve and protect" on them. For police agencies, it's not just a motto, it's the way they would like to enhance their interactions with the general public.

Perhaps Sam Walton of Wal-Mart said it best, "There is only one boss: the customer. And he can fire everyone in the company from the chairman on down; simply by spending his money somewhere else."

Why even cover this? As professionals we already know this. However, the lack of great service or communication may cause someone to feel things that ultimately may turn a calm situation into one where you feel your safety is in jeopardy.

Clearly customer service is very important. Many organizations employ some type of program such as "Service Excellence" and "Customer First" among many others.

What is Customer Service?

Depending on whom you ask, customer service can mean different things to people and organizations. However, to put it in a nutshell, it is the formation of a relationship between the individual customer and a company. Customers are made to feel special and will oftentimes return to the company to purchase additional goods and services and tend to remain loyal for their needs and perhaps recommend the company to others based on their experiences. In my book "How to Game Change Personal Service: Seven Principles," (available on Amazon.com), the author guides you in some out of the box ways to raise the service bar and keep customers happy, engaged and always asking for you.

How is Customer Service Accomplished?

> Going above and beyond customer expectations.
> Making something routine or mundane extraordinary.
> Being knowledgeable in your products and services.
> Professionalism.
> Bring something extra to the table.
> Finding other ways bring the customer experience to another level.
> Treat customers as if they were your own family.
> Finding answers and resolving problems.

Customers have many expectations and for those of us who have worked in the service industry for a while knows that the "customer is always right." We all wish to be treated fairly and with kindness, however, there are times when the customer will be very demanding and no matter what is done to correct the issue or how a situation is explained, the customer may treat you with disdain and state they will never return or report you to management. It is very important that you do not lose your cool, be argumentative, emotional or feel resentment. As long as you are acting in a professional manner and have done everything possible to turn a bad situation into a positive one, the next logical step would be to ask for management assistance. Another alternative would be to find the answer even if you do not know what it is. Let them know this so they know you are doing everything you can to help. While no one wants to hear "I pay your salary," in the overall scheme of things they do indirectly by buying goods and services from your employer or client.

As stated earlier, customers want to feel special and have a great experience!

How Do We Do This?

> There must be a level of trust between the customer and the company. In private security, the client, employees, visitors and others will hold you, the Private Officer, to a level of dependability and promise that you will perform your duties effectively.
> Public Safety and Private Officers must be responsive to customers' needs. The author will quantify this by stating that responsiveness is based on priorities and emergency situations. Outside of these circumstances, every effort must be made to answer customer questions, concerns and needs expeditiously and with a positive attitude.

➢ Demonstrating empathy will go a long way in how customers will feel toward you and the organization you represent. Even if you find yourself in an adversarial situation, there may be room for caring, particularly for a victim of a crime or perhaps a person who has lost something of value. On the flip side, a subject who has been apprehended or is being detained deserves some level of respect. Everyone has a reason for doing something.

➢ Perhaps the most important way to convey customer service is through company and personal assurances.

Studies have shown that great customer care produces higher job satisfaction, boosts morale, continued business success and higher revenue, not to mention safety.

Above and Beyond:

➢ Only by interacting with customers will you or the company know what level of satisfaction has been reached.

➢ Customers must believe you are sincere and trustworthy and therefore have confidence in your abilities, services and product knowledge.

➢ Be sure your visitors and customers have a positive experience even in unlikely circumstances.

➢ Be approachable! Your demeanor should be professional and yet individuals should feel comfortable around you.

➢ Do everything in your power to resolve issues. If concerns cannot be resolved immediately, advise them you will get back with a resolution or follow the next step.

➢ Treat everyone with due respect and with equality - all concerns should be treated equally.

➢ We should reflect a culture of value and commitment on behalf of the employer or client. What people see on the outside will determine what they believe will be in the inside.

Who Are Our Customers?

Everyone who interacts with us is a customer or potential customer. It's for this reason that treating everyone fairly and with respect is so important.

All businesses have two (2) types of customers:

External:

Any paying or non-paying customer who benefits from the goods or services provided. Private Officers are in the business of providing a safe and secure environment for persons legitimately entering a property. Indirectly however, they are the face of the company they are representing.

Internal:

Other colleagues, departments and staff who assists you in helping make the customer experience positive. This is a two (2) way street. It is for this reason that communications with others is so vital. Everyone is a stakeholder!

The First Impression

We all want to make a great first impression whether for a job interview, a first date or meeting a possible client for the first time. First impressions are often lasting impressions. It is this impression that will determine whether external or internal customers wish to further a relationship with your employer, client and even yourself.

What Makes for a Good Impression?

We have all heard that "you can't judge a book by its cover." We all try our best not too. Customers will undoubtedly look at the cover and if they like what they see will make a closer inspection. It's important to keep in mind that outwardly projecting confidence is the first step in keeping yourself and others safe.

There will be customers who will not appreciate what you are attempting to do, no matter how polite and courteous you are. As long as you act professional and strive to resolve issues, no one can argue your level of professionalism.

Ethical Considerations, Values and Integrity

Ethics and personal integrity is everything both in our personal and professional lives. We have all been taught right from wrong at an early age. However, we need to understand why it is so important to be ethical and have integrity. Professionals should understand how integrity and values affect our job performance, responsibilities and ultimately respect.

Every industry and profession has its own code of ethics. I have found that by adding this chapter to our training, many crises can be averted in the first place if people believe you are trustworthy and you value the person with whom you are working with on many levels.

What is Ethics?

Ethics deals with right and wrong conduct, what we should do and what we should refrain from doing. Other disciplines such as the law and theology also take into consideration certain behaviors.

The law is concerned with rules enacted by society and that effect with geographical boundaries. Theology concerns its self with the study of God and God's attributes, religious truth, divinity and personal relationship between God and human.

Many large companies, healthcare organizations and government entities, among others, have a code of ethics/conduct and a dedicated office, person or committee to oversee and investigate ethical concerns and dispositions. In addition, most professional associations, regardless of field or industry, have a code of ethics that all members must adhere, to remain in good standing.

Why Does Society Have Ethical Concerns?

Ethics are used by individuals and organizations as a "checks and balances" against society's perception of distrust even if none exists. We have all heard of the "Golden Rule" do unto others as you would have done to you."

Terminology:

Ethics: Moral principles or set of values that define or direct us to the right choice.

Crime: An offense (or criminal offense) is an act not only harmful to an individual but to society as well. It is an act against a community represented by the state, a "public wrong." These acts are forbidden and punishable by laws.

Embezzlement: One or more persons dishonestly retrieving assets for the purpose of converting or stealing from an organization or person whom the assets were entrusted to.

There are several types of embezzlement:

➤ Fraud.
➤ Criminal conversion.
➤ Property.
➤ Of person(s)
➤ Lawful possession.

Utilitarianism: The morally right action is the one which brings more good than bad to all persons involved - the greater good.

Morality: Principles or rules of right conduct or the distinction between right and wrong.

Egoism: The morally right action is the one which produces the greatest good for the individual

Categorical Imperative: The morally correct action that is performed from duty alone rather than inclination.

Divine Command: The morally correct action conforms to the commandments and teachings of the religious person's God - the action originates in the will of God.

Integrity: Adhering to moral and ethical principles through honesty. In other words, "doing the right thing when no one is watching."

Values: Influence on a person's behavior and attitude that serves as a broad guideline in all situations.

Loyalty: State or quality of a person's faithfulness to commitments or obligations.

Betrayal: Deceive, corrupt or misguide a person or organization.

Bribery: The criminal and ethical offense of offering, giving, soliciting, accepting something of value in exchange for influencing the action of a person or entity, public or private.

Kickback: A percentage of an asset, usually monetary, given to a person in a position of influence as payment for making the income possible - unethical, improper and in many cases illegal.

Transparency: Performing actions that others can easily see the operations.

It is important to keep in mind that no one (1) principle can address every single situation!

Character:

> Trustworthiness: Deserving confidence, honesty, faithfulness, dependability and reliability.
> Respect: Sense of worth of another person, personal quality or ability.
> Responsibility: Accountable for something in a person's power or control.
> Fairness: Free from bias or injustice. The ability to treat everyone in the same manner without "playing" favorites.
> Caring: A state of mind in which an individual is anxious, worried or concerned with attentive things.
> Citizenship: The character and behaviors of an individual or organization viewed as a member of society.

Ethical Principles:

> Be trustful.
> Keep an open mind.
> Meet obligations - honor all obligations and commitments.
> Be respectful.

Many organizations and professional associations adopt a formal Code of Ethics document that members must adhere to or face consequences such as termination from employment or terminating one's membership. The logic behind the code is to allow such profession or industry the opportunity to "police" themselves rather than have more governmental involvement. In addition, good public relations on behalf of the industry, association and company go a long way in retaining good talent and consumer confidence. Therefore, rather than have society perceive it as an "understanding," unwritten rule," corporate culture," or "consensus," it is codified to signal professionalism and quality.

A Code of Ethics provides employees, members and others with guidelines for making ethical choices in how they conduct their responsibilities.

Keep in mind that ethical violations are not necessarily legal wrong doings. Consequences such as terminating an employee can be difficult unless there is an "employment at will" policy and such decisions are backed by state and federal law under the circumstances.

General Code of Ethics (generic - does not reflect any one organization):

> To accept the responsibilities and obligations freely in my role as a professional.
> To conduct myself with honesty, integrity and to adhere to the highest moral principles in performing my duties.
> To be faithful, diligent and dependable in discharging my responsibilities - to uphold the laws, policies and procedures to protect the rights of others.
> Observe the truth, be prudent and accurate without allowing personal feelings, friendships or prejudices to influence my judgments or actions.
> To report to my superiors any violations of the law or of my employer and/or client's policies.

Be true to yourself and others. Mutual respect is earned.

Training

Every profession and every industry has certain training standards. At one point or another we have studied and passed a licensing exam or attended employer training upon being hired. Some of it might have been in a class setting or perhaps hands-on training. Either way training is a great thing. Unfortunately we just don't get enough of it. Why even talk about this and how does this affect your personal safety?

Simply put, practice makes perfect.

It's common knowledge that law enforcement, firefighters and Emergency Medical Services (EMS) personnel train regularly. Advances in techniques and equipment are always emerging and first responders must be on top of their game. It's about continually being proficient because you never know when your training will be called upon.

I also believe that everyone should be trained and prepared to face any event that may occur. Remember, it was stated earlier that public safety professionals can't be everywhere at once so it's imperative that you take personal safety and related training seriously.

Training can be delivered in many formats, such as this book or even online. Perhaps the best option is classroom based with an instructor certified in the subject matter. If you or your company plan to hire an instructor be sure they are qualified and ask about their professional experience. You may want to take the extra step and ask for a list of their clients. If a list is provided, call a few of them and ask about the training and the level of satisfaction received. Perform due diligence and research the best fit for you. A great instructor will have the participants well engaged and allow for questions after the training.

Training should not be considered a luxury, rather a necessity. Employees sometimes don't want to be bothered with something they believe they will never use or is a waste of time. For this reason alone, it's important to get buy in from the staff and the management as well. The case has to be made as to why the training is necessary and to stress that safety is everyone's responsibility. Unfortunately many believe that training has to be expensive or fear there will be a loss of productivity (i.e. work hours, days off, etc.).

There are companies out there that mandate quarterly or yearly training and refreshers mainly via online. The author strongly recommends you enroll in a self defense education course to assist you in protecting yourself until someone can respond to your call for help. Never assume that you can talk your way out of a situation.

There are several ways that training can be productive and inexpensive. This works best when all levels of management and employees are represented including other office locations if applicable.

The first is a table top exercise. This only requires participants in a room at a table. Once the participants have gathered, a moderator will present a scenario to the others that can range from a natural disaster to medical emergency and anything in between. The moderator will generally present limited facts of the scenario and then will allow the participants to begin talking out the various steps in resolving the emergency. A sharp moderator's job is to add more problems to the scenario as the resolution progresses. This makes the scenario more realistic to what could actually happen. Participants may ask the moderator questions about anything but he/she may choose to give additional information at their discretion. A successful conclusion to this exercise is when all possible options have been exhausted and explored, even if the participants believe they have failed. The bottom line is that everyone understands what could happen, the process to resolve it realistically and be prepared for any given situation. Keep a record of who participated, what the scenario was and what could use improving. These details will come in handy at a later date. It is strongly recommended these exercises be conducted at least once every quarter.

Perhaps one of the most important forms of training that is practical and adds some realism are fire drills and safety evacuations. In this type of training, employer policies and local and state codes must be considered so everyone knows how to employ this exercise. Local fire codes may dictate that fire drills take place one a month, a quarter, semi-annually or annually. This all depends on the type of building structure you are in and how people are in it at any given time. Some facilities, because of the nature of their business, seek professional accreditations and must follow the standards set forth by them under their safety assessments.

Schools and healthcare facilities are typical entities that are governed by these rules.

Depending on the jurisdiction, fire alarm activations may not necessarily mean an automatic evacuation. In a healthcare setting for example, staff are trained to "defend in place" meaning during an alarm activation, rather than attempting to evacuate all the patients, which is time consuming and logistically difficult, staff will "evacuate" horizontally first then vertical if need be. Generally, many of their walls and doors are fire rated to over two hours in the event a rescue must be performed.

For our purpose here however, we will make the assumption that your policy and local codes dictate the facility be evacuated.

I have heard many excuses as to why drills should not take place:

> It's cold/hot outside.
> It's raining.
> I'm busy, have a meeting, on a conference call, etc.
> Nothing will happen here.
> That's what police and fire are for.

I have conducted numerous fire drills in many different facilities and have heard it all. Remember, it's your personal safety we're talking about here. It's always in your best interest to cooperate and learn from these training sessions.

The process:

Fire and evacuation drills are most successful when the least amount of people knows about it. Real emergencies will not announce themselves before happening. Depending on whether your office is located in a large building shared with other business occupants or a stand- alone space, your drill training process may vary. In larger occupancies, the facilities or security team may conduct the drill and you will simply follow the instructions given by them.

In an ideal drill scenario, the local fire and police departments and EMS are asked to participate with you. They have the experience and knowledge to advise you of where things went well and what could use improving. Whether the fire department participates or not, you should contact them to let them know you will be performing a fire drill and the "pull station" will be activated. It's also a good idea to call the alarm company associated with the facility as well. Be sure to call them back at the completion of the training. It is also <u>imperative</u> the person who is activating the alarm system know how to reset it as well.

Depending on the size of the facility, the person should pick out a different pull station location for each drill. In general, once the activation has occurred (horns and strobes) employees and visitors should evacuate the building or space in an orderly fashion via the designated routes out of the facility, assisting others who are disabled or have difficulty moving and meet at a designated area for a head count. Although this only a drill, treat it like the real thing. There should be a separate person within your group who will make notations of the evacuation and make sure everyone is accounted for.

At a later time, be sure everyone gets together to discuss how the training went. Be sure to reiterate how important safety is and why training is necessary. Included in this briefing should be the clarification of everyone's responsibilities should a real emergency occur. Documentation is very important and should be kept in a safe place.

Professionals should take into consideration becoming trained and certified in CPR/AED as well as first aid from a certified instructor. Many offices and buildings now employ AEDs (Automated External Defibrillator).

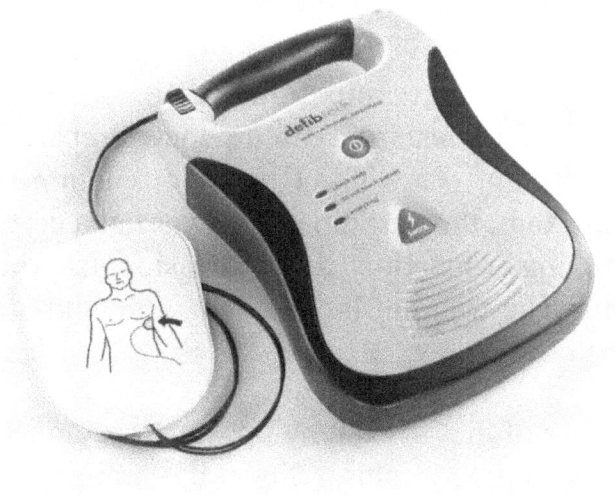

As I stated earlier, personal safety begins with you. In an emergency seconds count. Having trained people to help during an incident will go a long way in mitigating the situation. Contact the American Red Cross or the American Heart Association.

Many companies contract with vendors to provide training via online software programs. In most cases, each employee will have their own username and password. This method allows staff to receive their training at anytime that is flexible for them and still be in compliance. It also retains information such as test scores so remedial action can be taken to further the learning and retention process. Training can range from active shooter to disaster management. For an additional fee vendors can also customize the training that best suits your goals.

Colleges and universities offer safety lectures from noted law enforcement and security professionals, many free of charge on their campuses. They also offer these lectures via streaming live, webinar format or recorded videos. The values these lectures bring are often worth the time to watch and listen. Some institutions of higher education also provide non-students the ability to sign up for training on their website free of charge.

If you're looking for training videos on various safety topics, look no further than the internet. Major search engines will guide you to videos posted by training companies and experts in the field. Simply search for "training videos" or "safety videos" and let the training begin. It's all at your fingertips and best of all they can be watched on any device with internet connection.

If you prefer online training, the author recommends turning to the federal government, namely the Emergency Management Institute (EMI) of the Federal Emergency Management Agency (FEMA). Under their Independent Study program, the agency provides numerous training courses available to the general public covering a range of topics from Emergency Preparedness to Community Emergency Response Team (CERT). Upon completion of the course and successfully passing an exam, the participant is awarded a certificate which may be applied toward continuing education for professionals who have to maintain certification credentials. The training is free. You can find additional information at: https://training.fema.gov/is/

Attending training outside of the office may appear to be an inconvenience to some but in reality it can be a good thing. Since the training you receive will be invaluable, the likelihood of office distractions will be kept to a minimum outside of texts and phone calls. Many of the instructors the author has worked with will usually ask participants to silence devices. Depending on the length of the training, they may also give periodic breaks and lunch to give you an opportunity to check in with the office and to refresh your mind.

Be sure to investigate local resources within your town or city. Many police departments host a citizen's academy for the general public. These programs are very informative and give the public a behind the scenes look at how the department operates as well as dispensing safety and security tips. Most of these academies are six to eight weeks and cover a lot of information but is well worth the time investment and generally free. Additionally, some police departments offer self defense classes free of charge or for a nominal fee.

Your local fire department and EMS are also invaluable training resources. Many offer free fire and safety tips training for the general public. Career and volunteer firefighters and EMS personnel will also stop by any facility to recommend safety upgrades. If you have a real interest in public safety you may want to consider becoming a volunteer firefighter or Emergency Medical Technician.

Although the training is serious, the author prefers a relaxed environment in which participants feel comfortable learning and asking questions. No question is silly, keep that in mind.

During the author's tenure in security management, one of the best training methods we employed was media reports. The author would pick one incident reported on the news and during our monthly meeting with subordinates we would discuss the incident and play out what could have been done. The exercise was timed to only fifteen minutes but a lot of training came out of it. This is an excellent method for professionals with limited time and can easily be done at the end of each meeting.

In the end, training can be accomplished in many different ways but above all it's important to get management buy in. However, it's up to you to take your personal safety seriously enough that it becomes second nature. Make the time for training – your life or the lives of others could depend on it.

Choosing to Arm Yourself:

Firearms:

This book is all about your personal safety and choosing to arm yourself with a weapon is by no means an easy decision. There are many factors that should be taken into consideration if you plan on purchasing and carrying a firearm. While the 2nd Amendment to the U.S. Constitution states," A well regulated militia, being necessary to the security of a free state, the right of the people to keep and bear arms, shall not be infringed," there are certain steps that must be taken in order to be properly trained and armed. The Connecticut Department of Emergency Services and Public Protection, Connecticut State Police, Special Licensing and Firearms Unit outlines the following procedures to legally obtain a pistol permit:

As of the writing of this book, the statutes are current. For additional information, appropriate forms and applications go to: www.ct.gov and click on the "Firearms" tab.

The Special Licensing and Firearms Unit is responsible for the issuance of state pistol permits. Applicants for a state pistol permit must first apply for, and be granted a local pistol permit. A local pistol permit may be obtained from the police chief in the town in which you reside:

Connecticut statute reads in part:

Sec. 29-36f. Eligibility certificate for pistol or revolver. (a) Any person who is twenty-one years of age or older may apply to the Commissioner of Emergency Services and Public Protection for an eligibility certificate for a pistol or revolver.

(b) The Commissioner of Emergency Services and Public Protection shall issue an eligibility certificate unless said commissioner finds that the applicant: (1) Has failed to successfully complete a course approved by the Commissioner of Emergency Services and Public Protection in the safety and use of pistols and revolvers including, but not limited to, a safety or training course in the use of pistols and revolvers available to the public offered by a law enforcement agency, a private or public educational institution or a firearms training school, utilizing instructors certified by the National Rifle Association or the Department of Energy and Environmental Protection and a safety or training course in the use of pistols or revolvers conducted by an instructor certified by the state or the National Rifle Association; (2) has been convicted of a felony or of a violation of section 21a-279 or

section 53a-58, 53a-61, 53a-61a, 53a-62, 53a-63, 53a-96, 53a-175, 53a-176, 53a-178 or 53a-181d; (3) has been convicted as delinquent for the commission of a serious juvenile offense, as defined in section 46b-120; (4) has been discharged from custody within the preceding twenty years after having been found not guilty of a crime by reason of mental disease or defect pursuant to section 53a-13; (5) (A) has been confined in a hospital for persons with psychiatric disabilities, as defined in section 17a-495, within the preceding sixty months by order of a probate court; or (B) has been voluntarily admitted on or after October 1, 2013, to a hospital for persons with psychiatric disabilities, as defined in section 17a-495, within the preceding six months for care and treatment of a psychiatric disability and not solely for being an alcohol-dependent person or a drug-dependent person as those terms are defined in section 17a-680; (6) is subject to a restraining or protective order issued by a court in a case involving the use, attempted use or threatened use of physical force against another person, including an ex parte order issued pursuant to section 46b-15 or section 46b-16a; (7) is subject to a firearms seizure order issued pursuant to subsection (d) of section 29-38c after notice and hearing; (8) is prohibited from shipping, transporting, possessing or receiving a firearm pursuant to 18 USC 922(g)(4); or (9) is an alien illegally or unlawfully in the United States.

An eligibility certificate is issued pursuant to <u>C.G.S. 29-36f</u> through <u>29-36i</u>. It entitles the holder to purchase a firearm and transport same to their residence or place of business. <u>It does not entitle the holder to carry a pistol or revolver on their person.</u>

You will also be required to submit to a background investigation, criminal history check and submit photographs and fingerprints in connection with your application.

The issuing authority has 90 days to review your application and issue an approval or denial. In the event that they deny your application, they must provide you a written explanation listing the basis for denial. A denial may be appealed to the **Board of Firearm Permit Examiners** *as provided under <u>C.G.S. 29-32b</u>.*

You are **required** *to complete a handgun safety course, which must consist of no less than the NRA's "Basic Pistol Course," prior to submitting the application. The NRA's* **"Home Firearms Safety Course"** *and* **"First Steps Pistol Orientation Program"** *are* **not approved courses***.*

Live fire is also required. *Computer-generated programs, dry-fire, other simulated shooting tools, plastic bullets, air guns or any other alternatives are not* *acceptable. Students must fire a semi-automatic pistol or revolver. Any questions should be referred to the Special Licensing and Firearms Unit.*

You will also be required to submit to a background investigation, criminal history check and submit fingerprints and photographs in connection with your application. The licensing statute also contains a "suitability clause" which provides that the issuing authority may deny such application, if it determines that the applicant is not a suitable person to possess or carry a pistol or revolver. The suitability clause applies both to the issuance of new permits and revocation of existing permits. Applicants must provide proof you are legally and lawfully in the United States, such as a birth certificate, or U.S. Passport. Legal Alien Residents must provide Alien Registration numbers and 90-day proof of residency. Naturalized citizens require proof of citizenship.

Once you have successfully applied and received your firearms permit, owning and carrying them is a tremendous responsibility. Keep in mind that you must be properly trained with the particular firearm you purchase and plan on carrying. Any subsequent firearms that you purchase you must be trained on.

If you plan to carry, it's always best to conceal it in an appropriate gun holder. Women may choose to carry in their purse however you must keep the purse in sight or locked up. Open carry will only invite others to call law enforcement at the sight of a firearm. Private property owners and employers have the right to ban firearms on their properties regardless of the fact that you are licensed. However recent court cases say a firearm may be kept in a vehicle when the vehicle is parked on the property.

Do not let anyone hold or handle your firearm for any reason. Accidents will happen and there could be legal consequences that follow. Also, there is no need for you to display your firearm unless you believe you are in imminent danger and must use force as a last resort. The exception to this would be in the event a law enforcement officer asks for it along with your license in the course of their legal duties. You must have your firearms license on you at all times when you are carrying!

It is strongly recommended that you purchase a safe for your firearm at your residence, especially if there are children. Also be sure to purchase a gun lock which will make the firearm inoperable should anyone try to use it. Keep the weapon well maintained and attend training outlined in your paperwork, license and statutes.

Knives:

One thing you should never leave home without is a small pocket knife, preferably the Swiss Army type that includes all the gadgets such a screwdriver, bottle opener, etc – you get the idea. Having them on you is advantageous because they are discreet and have many uses.

Connecticut law is very specific as to what is defined as a dangerous weapon and the consequences associated with them:

"State law defines certain knives as dangerous weapons and, with minor exceptions, makes it illegal to carry them on one's person or in a vehicle. The law does not prohibit mere possession of these weapons (i.e., possession in one's residence, according to the state Supreme Court). And it does not address sales and purchases.

Under the law, dangerous weapons are (1) dirk knives, (2) switch knives, (3) stilettos, (4) any knife that has an automatic spring release device that releases a blade from the handle longer than one and one-half inches, and (5) any knife that has a blade with an edged portion four inches or longer.

Illegally carrying a dangerous weapon on one's person is punishable by a fine of up to $500, imprisonment for up to three years, or both (CGS § 53-206(a)). Illegally carrying it in a vehicle is punishable by a fine of up to $1,000, imprisonment for up to five years, or both (CGS § 29-38).

The law does not contain any provisions specifically addressing antique knives."

The bottom line is knives are weapons and as such are regulated much like firearms due to its ease of concealment and use. Most of us don't carry these types of knives in our everyday lives but criminals may. If you are approached by an individual with a knife, follow the same principles outlined under "firearms." There are training firms who specifically train individuals on response and safety to dangerous weapons. Should you decide to attend this type of training, you should always follow the principles I have outlined throughout the book. Even with proper training, nothing is guaranteed because circumstances vary incident to incident.

Less Than Lethal Option:

It's understandable that some people may not be comfortable with carrying and using a firearm. You may want to consider a less than lethal option such as pepper spray. It's available to the general public and legal in all states including Connecticut. However there may be local restrictions on size and concentration. This option is a good alternative because it's easily concealable on the person. The most popular version of pepper spray is the keychain. There are generally no laws with restrictions where you can carry it. There are federal laws however that prohibits this at security check points or on aircraft. Common sense would dictate that you would not bring this through a Security Transportation Administration screening like any other weapon. If you insist on bringing it, place it into checked luggage.

How it Works:

"Pepper spray's active ingredient is OC or oleoresin capsicum. The OC is derived from Cayenne peppers these are some of the hottest peppers in the world. Unlike MACE or tear gas, which are irritants, pepper spray OC is an inflammatory agent. Contact with mucous membranes (eyes, nose, throat and lungs) causes immediate dilation of the capillaries. This can result in temporary blindness and instant inflammation of the breathing tube tissues and systematically cuts of all but life support breathing. OC also will create an intense burning sensation on the surface of the skin. However, OC will cause no lasting after effects. The effects last from 15 to 60 minutes. Because OC is an inflammatory agent and not an irritant it is effective on those who feel no pain such as psychotics and those under the influence of drugs or alcohol" (Crime911 – Hazen & Associates).

As with any or self-defense weapon, you should only use it if you believe you are in imminent danger. The use of pepper spray other than its intended use for your safety is considered a crime.

If a threat exists and you must release the spray, make every attempt to give yourself and the other person some space if possible so there is less chance of feeling the effects. Aim for the facial area, particularly the eyes. Spray one or two bursts and get away from the area. In some cases the effect of the pepper spray may take a few moments before the full reaction hits them. Keep your eyes on the other person. You may have to spray again if it appears it doesn't work the first time. Be sure to move every time you spray. Keep in mind that pepper spray may not have the desired effect on individuals who are intoxicated or high on drugs.

Be sure to test the spray periodically. They do have expirations. Training on the proper use and effects are always recommended.

Stun Guns:

Under Connecticut law, electronic defense weapons, such as stun guns, are classified as dangerous or deadly weapons. With limited exceptions, the law prohibits people from carrying these weapons on their person or in motor vehicles.

Stun guns are less than lethal weapons capable if temporarily immobilizing someone via an electric pulse which is not capable of causing death or serious physical injury. More commonly called or known as "Tasers," law enforcement officers deploy them in situations where less than lethal is optimal in subduing or halting physical aggression.

The author strongly suggests that whichever way you choose to be armed, you comply with all mandated state and local laws with regards to training and possession. Be sure to re-qualify and continually train even if you are comfortable with your knowledge base.

"Take advantage of what you are able to learn."

Dan Sinisi

My Thoughts

Support Your Profession:

What does it even mean to support your profession? We already support it by the very fact we are employed within it, right? That's partially right. However, there's more to it.

The most important way to support you profession or industry is to be proud of what you do and what you or your employer have accomplished. Speaking negatively about your job, your boss or employer does nothing but generate bad vibes for those with whom you are relating this too. Many employees tend to find fault with their employer or industry as a whole because of the position they are in. Perhaps you believe that a raise is justifiable or you should be promoted because you've been at the company for many years. These are good reasons to be upset but it doesn't justify the negative portrayal you may be spreading.

Not too long ago I wrote about being a professional. Professionalism means you are willing to see things from all sides and be knowledgeable in your skills set. This also includes how you handle disappointments and what you may perceive to be wrongs committed against you and your colleagues. It's easy to say don't act on your emotions, after all we are human. The author is saying you have the power, if you so choose, to change things if you place your energy on concentrating on the positive while encouraging change through positive means. Remember that speaking negatively not only leaves a bad taste for the employer and industry but also will be a reflection on you as well. Imagine for a moment you work for a certain company and said company has decided to forgo raises because sales were down. You decide to take to social media and let loose your tirade. Little did you know the company would be offering other perks in lieu of a raises. At this point, the damage has been done. Believe me, those posts are there for everyone to see, even those employed at said company. Being a professional means thinking things through and realizing what consequences might arise. Should you decide to apply to another company, you can almost be sure social media posts will be part of the background check.

Placing your employer in a negative light while speaking to clients, visitors or others you come into contact with only hurts you in the end. Yes, the company will be perceived as one people don't want to do business with but ultimately you will be looked upon as unprofessional. You would be doing a great disservice to yourself because a person you believe is not associated with the company may actually be a company executive you do not know. Your words and attitude are sure to go beyond your conversation.

Joining a professional association is perhaps the best way to support your profession. While most of them do charge a nominal membership fee, the benefits usually outweigh the investment. Many of the organizations are in the business of placing their industry or profession in a positive light by advancing their agenda on behalf of professionals and companies. Many offer training to members and will keep you in the loop about legislation that may affect you or your career. They generally have a vast networking capability to which they call upon to collectively support the association's mission. I am a member of several organizations and have found them to be very beneficial. They are my voice. It is much easier when a professional organization who represents many people takes on the responsibility of advancing the industry on our behalf.

Advocate for your profession by becoming involved in one of these associations. It's easy to sit back and blame everyone. If you want change, you have to be part of that change.

Many associations also offer professional certifications. Earning a certification not only helps you as a professional but in the grander scheme of things support your profession as well. Professionalism and positive reinforcement are essential if we want to advance our causes.

You are in charge of your own destiny. If your position is that you have a greater mission and that you want to make a difference while earning a more stable salary, do something positive. Perhaps go back to school, be willing to learn new skills at work, and learn from other people by asking questions. Employers are always looking for positive people that can solve problems rather than complain about them.

Leadership: What it Means to Me:

I think we all can agree that at some point in our lives we all aspire to be leaders whether in our professional or personal lives. I have read numerous books, articles and posts that broach the subject. Each person has one opinion or another. I have worked with many professionals throughout my career and in the end, it appears that a leader, according to them, is a person that is leading a pack, head of something or other and perhaps better educated.

One day my son returned home from school and was very excited. He was chosen to be the "leader" for the week in his first grade class. Naturally I asked him what that meant. Apparently the teacher randomly selects students to "help" the teacher with the class, i.e. make sure everyone is in line, that students quiet down when the teacher is speaking, etc. I was amused since my son is only seven years old. Nevertheless, I was happy for him. I then asked him how he would lead his friends and students. His answer was a classic that I had heard before. "I'm in charge and I tell them what to do." I answered him, "your teacher asked you to be a leader, not a boss. He had a hard time understanding the difference but he eventually got the concept I was explaining to him. It's always difficult explaining something to a young child when something is not explained fully. Perhaps the teacher did go over what the leader does and he didn't quite understand.

Leadership is not about being a boss or being in charge of something or people. It's about the qualities a person has that makes them aspiring, emulated and sought after. Sometimes it comes naturally and sometimes it doesn't. It's a quality I look for in the people that I encounter throughout my professional and personal circles.

I never thought of myself much as leader until I was promoted into security management at a local hospital after six years of service. The position included additional responsibilities including overseeing the staff. I was excited at the prospect of being in charge and being able to make some changes. The new position required me to wear a suit and tie rather than the uniform. What I really needed and didn't know was leadership skills. It dawned on me one afternoon when a violent patient was brought into the Emergency Department. He had assaulted the police officers, paramedics and others prior to coming in. I was in my office doing some paperwork and checking emails and I heard an emergency "stat" call come over the radio. Instinctively, I ran out of the office and assisted my officers in the takedown and control of the patiently safely. My director pulled me to the side after the incident and said a few choice words to me about getting physically involved in what the security officers were supposed to be doing. I simply answered him that I was just as willing to get my hands dirty as the officers. I became a leader and earned respect of the staff, something that was always mentioned among us. I understood what it meant and lead by example. I kept everyone to the same standards. Officers were empowered to be leaders and lead by example as well. We became a model department.

Several years later I was appointed as a Security Manager for a large commercial real estate complex. I had a much larger staff spread over six different properties. The very first thing I did was have several mandatory staff meetings with all the officers. I wrote one word on the whiteboard behind me: "Leadership." I explained it very clearly what it meant to me and that I lived by it. I was willing to do their jobs if need be to accomplish goals. The one thing they were never to say to me was "you don't know what it's like to do this job, work these hours, etc." Simply explained to them was that I had been there and done that and perhaps more. We were a team and we would move forward as one.

Leadership is a willingness to lead by example, be a team player and empower those who feel they have to be a boss to get things done to care and be willing to help others succeed. As I eventually explained to my son, being a leader means helping out, reaching out and not expecting to receive praise and credit. It's about working together, sharing knowledge and understanding.

Your Personal Safety Belongs to You:

The title says it all. Amazingly a majority of people would offer a different opinion. Let me start off by saying many communities have their own police department, fire department and EMS agencies. In some areas private security exists to provide added protection at a specific site. Yes, they exist to serve and protect, to patrol our neighborhoods or respond to our calls for help and assistance. As you can imagine these are very busy people and calls for service continue to climb yearly. The reality is they can't be everywhere at once.

Traditionally law enforcement has been viewed as a reactionary force rather than a proactive one. While this is true, they have made great strides in being more proactive by starting or enhancing popular programs such citizen police academies, community policing initiatives and social media engagements. I believe engagement is the first step to any successful program.

In a perfect world this would be enough and we would count on our men and women in uniform to not only save the day but also prevent things from happening in the first place. They risk their lives every day to keep us safe and often go above and beyond the call of duty. I know first-hand. However, being that we do live in the real world, ultimately the safety of ourselves belongs to us individually. Yes, we are responsible for our own safety. So what does that exactly mean?

I am not advocating that we all arm ourselves with firearms and become like the Old West. However I am advocating to know what you have available to keep yourself safe.

The most important weapon you have is your senses. Use them to your advantage. Look around you. Be aware of your surroundings. What do you see, hear or smell? Your senses will let you know that something isn't right. If you can safely call for help, do so. If that's not possible be prepared to take some kind of action.

Be proactive. You may want to consider taking self defense training or other safety and security related training. Learn how to use a fire extinguisher and become trained in CPR and AED. Sign up for any training your first responder agencies may provide. Many of these classes are free or at very little cost.

Keep the amount of information you post limited on social media regarding your whereabouts, where you are checking in or when you are away or on vacation. There are people out there looking for the right opportunity to commit crimes. Don't supply them with information that may work against you.

Keep in communication with your family or close friends especially if you are alone and more importantly in an unfamiliar area. Trust your gut. If something doesn't feel right, it probably isn't.

Lastly, follow tips and advice that first responder agencies put out. They are very informative and are intended to keep you abreast of what is happening and to keep you safe. You have a responsibility to keep yourself well informed and prepared.

First responders will do everything possible to keep you safe. Likewise, take the initiative and help them help you.

Be Careful with Social Media – On or Off the Job:

The internet is either a wonderful thing or a beast of burden depending on whom you ask. Personally, I think it's a terrific tool if used properly. The possibilities are endless from communication to shopping to reaching out globally and everything in between.

Perhaps though, we sometimes don't think of the consequences of our actions once we are online. There has been great debate recently of personnel posting opinions and comments on their social media. Sometimes these posts are not very flattering and go beyond incendiary. There is much frustration in this world and people have turned to social media to voice their anger. I believe everyone is entitled to an opinion. The lines become blurred however when the posts are from employees of a company where said posts could do harm to the reputation of said company or agency. At the center of the debate is whether posting online as an employee is a First Amendment right, whether the person is at work on the clock or is off duty.

Professionals should always be held to a higher standard, even off the clock. For this reason it's even more important to be careful what you post. With the internet being "infinite," posts can be seen by millions of people and possibly go viral. Many post things believing no one else may see it except in closed groups or one on one communications. Companies and agencies are constantly scanning the internet for information. All it takes is one share and there it goes through the vast internet. By this point you no longer have control of who sees it or even trying to stop the spread. Imagine getting pulled into the office having to explain what you wrote something not so nice about your boss. Remember also that companies and agencies look to social media as part of their background checks to see if you are a suitable fit.

I concede that having an open and honest debate is what makes this country great. However, when debate turns to bullying or other forms of harassing communication, it takes on a whole new level cyber safety and concern.

It's easier said than done. After all we are humans with emotions. However keep in mind that any negative posting could have employment consequences as well as legal ones. Your post could be influential in a positive or negative way. Use the internet and social media wisely.

Drills and Training are not Inconveniences:

As an elementary school student I can remember school officials conducting fire drills periodically and it was considered the norm. As a matter of fact every time we had one it gave us kids a chance to get away from our school work and be social. We never gave a second though to why we had these drills to begin with. It was explained to us but that was a lot of adult talk. Today schools continue to employ these drills as well as active shooter, earthquake and others. It's the reality of today.

It's important for us adults in the workplace as well. Many of us don't give a second thought about workplace violence, natural or manmade disasters until the very moment it happens. In my experience I have found that employees don't want to be bothered to participate in any drills especially if the weather is uncooperative or there is a security presence. Yes, security officers should be aware of their response and responsibilities but shouldn't be depended on totally for your safety. They will be very busy engaged and overwhelmed with what they are doing.

Safety is everyone's responsibility. That's the bottom line. It's for this very reason that participating in drills, whatever they may be, is so important. You're knowledge of what to do could save your life and the lives of others.

Drilling serves two purposes:

First, as I mentioned above, to be prepared for what to do and sometimes not to do is critical, especially in a life or death situation.

Secondly, it gives management and staff an opportunity to look for mistakes and what could use improvement. Training is key. For this reason accurate records need to be kept to ensure that any future training or remediation is based on realistic numbers and scenarios. Merely going through the motions and pre-filling out paperwork (as the author has seen) is doing a tremendous disservice to everyone in the workplace including visitors and vendors.

Employers should conduct scheduled and unscheduled drills with only a few people who will need to know about it to keep it as real as possible.

Conducting drills with the local police, fire and EMS does wonders to add realism to your staff training. They continually train and are most likely to participate if staffing levels permit and enough notice is given.

After any drill, set up a time to sit with staff and go over your findings, good and bad. Let them know why the drills are conducted and what steps will be taken to improve response. Allow staff to voice safety concerns and address. By doing this you are letting the staff buy in to their own safety. Likewise, staff should not be afraid to approach management with safety concerns at any time and should be given every opportunity whether through a formal program or informal communication such as email, letter or in person.

Documentation is very important. Keep all drill and training records up to date and available especially for public safety, risk manager and if the employer seeks accreditation from a recognized agency

Drills and training should not be a once a year and done deal. Make the extra effort and train as often as possible. Get into the mindset that practicing safety and conducting drills will benefit everyone.

Check Your Attitude at the Door:

It's happened to all us at one point or another. We walk into our place of employment in such a mood that staying out of the way is the best thing anyone encountering you can do.

I believe many of us have family or personal issues to contend with. Some are more complex than others. It may even be work related.

Depending on the type of person you are, your mood will dictate how your day will go and how you treat others. As a manager, I was known to tell subordinates to "check their attitude at the door" when they came on duty. Moodiness had no place at work. In a job that required skill and tact, an attitude problem was the last thing anyone needed. I would regularly tell staff that everyone they would encounter might be having their own issues and part of their job was to be sensitive and understanding of others.

I will admit it's not easy and have had some attitude adjusting of my own to do, but it was always before walking in the door.

The challenge has always been to separate personal and professional lives especially if we are on call, receiving business related phone calls or perhaps checking emails from home. In any of these instances the same rules apply.

One way that my staff found helpful in dealing with their mood was making myself available to meet with them confidentially and off the record. I found that by allowing them to vent and talk about whatever was bothering them helped a great deal even though an issue couldn't be solved. I wasn't a counselor or a professional therapist but was someone they could just talk too. By doing this, the I was showing they were not alone. For the most part it worked. Of course there will always be someone who will act the way they want regardless of how much you try to help them.

We all have bad days but in the end it's a matter of how you deal with it. Don't let your less than good mood dictate how things will go. Rise above it and move forward.

Be Aware of Your Surroundings:

Be aware of your surroundings! These are the last five words I use daily after signing on to social media platforms and greeting everyone. Outside of public safety, many people are truly unaware of what this phrase really means. For those of us who serve in public safety, you are very well versed and live by this mantra daily.

We all live a busy life. The hustle and bustle of our jobs, our personal lives, and even when we aren't doing much of anything, we don't give a second thought to what is going around us until something happens right then and there. Sometimes it's too late to react to or prevent what would happen. Case in point; in early 2016 in the Midwest, a robber had forced his way behind the counter of a convenience store, assaulted the female clerk and took the money out of the register drawer and fled. Let me clear, there may be certain times that you could do everything possible to react or try to prevent but the event occurs anyway. What makes this case among others unique is that the event was caught on surveillance camera and it clearly tells the story of what had transpired.

In the CCTV footage, a young lady is shown standing behind the counter of the store. Her eyes are fixated on her phone, not for a few seconds, not for a minute, but longer. She has no idea what is about to happen. A male emerges from what appears to be the front door of the store and rushes the counter. The clerk is immediately assaulted and unable to react to the event. The robber grabs the money and dashes out the door again. The entire event lasted just under thirty seconds. The clerk is left scared and helpless. I presume the police were called after.

In this scenario, the clerk was totally unprepared. She had no idea of what was going on around her. Could she have done something? It's hard to say. Some people react differently to various circumstances. The one sure thing is she was not aware of your surroundings.

This is just one example of what happens all the time. At one point or another we have all become guilty of this. It's simply reality. However, the reality is that it could work against us. For example, people crossing the street or driving while texting are all too common. Imagine for a moment you are in your car waiting for a traffic signal to turn green. You start texting or talking on the phone. The next thing you know you are being carjacked. What about the car turning the corner while you're texting and not paying attention. They came out of nowhere.

Having served in public safety and private security for a number of years, being aware of our surroundings is not only taught but becomes second nature on and off duty. Here's an example I use with our training participants: I was out with a few friends at a restaurant. The server attempted to sit the four of us at a middle table. While my friends had no issue with the table, I did and politely asked the server to sit us further down in a booth. He agreed. Prior to sitting, I called dibs on a particular seat. One of my friends became a little annoyed and asked me what the difference was in the seating arrangement. I told him clearly that I wanted a good view of the restaurant, to see what everyone was doing and most importantly who was entering and exiting the doors. After a puzzled look I further explained my position would give me an opportunity to scan and react to a possible event. Yes, I bring my training with me and no my friends are not in the public safety field. Anyone that goes out with me will already know this including my family.

Scanning your surroundings should also be second nature to you, anytime, anywhere. Complacency has no room in the world we live in. Pay attention to what is going on around you. It's one of the best ways of being least vulnerable.

The public safety campaign of "if you see something, say something" quantifies this. Be safe and be aware of your surroundings!

The Professional Inside Us:

If you have been employed in any occupation for a number of years most people would consider you a professional. You may also consider yourself a professional because you're good at what you do and the number of years you have been doing it. Perhaps you have a natural ability.

The Webster Dictionary defines professional as "Of or pertaining to a profession, or calling; conforming to the rules or standards of a profession; following a profession; as, professional knowledge; professional conduct."

We all want to be considered professionals, especially if we enjoy what we do.

Being a professional is not just simply saying you are one. A true professional is ethical in everything they do, not only on the job, but in their personal lives as well. While some may argue that earning a college degree makes a person more of a professional than others, there are individuals out there who are very knowledgeable and experienced enough to perform their respective responsibilities. Earning a college degree can be very rewarding in your career goals. However, there are also professional certifications that can just as easily help you attain your goals.

You want to be considered a professional by your peers, employer, and society in general? Act like one! A professional is a dedicated person who understands a person's or employer's needs and acts on them in an appropriate manner. A professional will seek out answers if they don't know something. A professional will not simply brush off a request or question if they feel it is not their job or area of expertise. A professional is always willing to learn something new or keep their skills sharp by seeking out training, whether through their employer or on their own. Joining a professional association may also boost your professionalism.

There is also one more aspect to being a professional - the attitude toward the profession and employment. A professional is confident and sincere and makes mistakes. Yes - we are human and as humans we do make mistakes. It should not be considered a weakness but rather an opportunity to improve yourself and learn. More often than not, you will be respected for seeking to correct a mistake. Treating your colleagues and others with respect and dignity will go a long way in showing others you are a professional.

Respect must be earned and being a professional is a very good start!

About the Author

Donato "Dan" Sinisi is a veteran public safety and private security management professional with over twenty-five years of experience in healthcare, corporate, and residential protection services and proudly serving in the volunteer fire service. He graduated Phi Theta Kappa from NCC with an Associate of Science in Criminal Justice Administration. Mr. Sinisi also earned the Certified Asset Protection Professional, Certified Advanced Healthcare Security Officer, Certified Homeland Security-IV, Certified Protection Officer Instructor, Certified Campus Security Specialist designations among others. He is also an approved State of Connecticut Security Officer Training Instructor as well as a certified and approved Management of Aggressive Behavior (MOAB®) Instructor.

Mr. Sinisi is a Founding Partner of Sound Training Group LLP and an Advisory Board Member of Private Officer International and contributes regularly to professional trade journals.

He is also the Author of "The Art of Private Patrol: What You Really Need to Know" and "How to Game Change Personal Service: Seven Principles."

Connect with me on social media:

Acknowledgements

A special thank you to Detective Desmond Ryan, Toronto Police Service (Retired) for his input and valuable assistance.